Teaching the
iGeneration

SECOND EDITION

Solution Tree | Press

a division of
Solution Tree

WILLIAM M. FERRITER / ADAM GARRY

555 North Morton Street
Bloomington, IN 47404
800.733.6786 (toll free) / 812.336.7700
FAX: 812.336.7790
email: info@solution-tree.com
solution-tree.com

Visit **go.solution-tree.com/technology** to download the reproducibles in this book.

Printed in the United States of America

19   18   17   16   15   1   2   3   4   5

Library of Congress Cataloging-in-Publication Data

Ferriter, William M.

   Teaching the Igeneration : five easy ways to introduce essential skills with Web 2.0 tools / William M. Ferriter and Adam Garry. -- Second edition.

      pages cm

   Includes bibliographical references and index.

   ISBN 978-1-936765-32-4 (perfect bound) 1. Web 2.0--Study and teaching. 2. Web-based instruction. 3. Internet in education. 4. Educational technology. I. Garry, Adam. II. Title.

   LB1044.87.F47 2015

   371.33'44678--dc23

                  2015003875

Solution Tree
Jeffrey C. Jones, CEO
Edmund M. Ackerman, President

Solution Tree Press
President: Douglas M. Rife
Associate Acquisitions Editor: Kari Gillesse
Editorial Director: Lesley Bolton
Managing Production Editor: Caroline Weiss
Production Editor: Rachel Rosolina
Proofreader: Ashante K. Thomas
Text Designers: Orlando Angel, Abigail Bowen, and Rian Anderson
Cover Designers: Orlando Angel and Abigail Bowen

To my beautiful daughter and wife, who I'll happily spend a lifetime loving. —Bill Ferriter

To my amazing son Michael, to my best friend Sarah, and in memory of my son Max, who are the inspiration for everything I do and love. —Adam Garry

Acknowledgments

Like all pieces of writing, this second edition of *Teaching the iGeneration* is the product of a thousand shared experiences. For Bill, those experiences began with Sheryl Nussbaum-Beach and John Norton, friends and colleagues from the Teacher Leaders Network. More than any single person, Sheryl has shaped Bill's thinking around good teaching and learning with technology—for adults and children alike. And more than any single person, John has shaped Bill's development as a writer and as a digital moderator. Their contributions to who Bill has become are immeasurable, rivaled only by the daily contributions made by the countless members of his personal learning network.

Bill's shared experiences continued with Mike Hutchinson, Marcy Russell, Emily Swanson, and Lyndsey Lowe, his long-time teammates and teaching partners at Salem Middle School in Apex, North Carolina. Constantly driven to grow as learners and leaders, they have never stopped imagining with Bill! Their willingness to dream about what could be—rather than get stuck in what is—has led to most of the lessons shared inside these pages. They are the quiet heroes of his professional career: constantly pushing, constantly prodding, constantly polishing, constantly improving.

Adam's shared experiences began many years ago in an elementary school in Pasco County. One person, John Mann, believed in him and invested the time to support his growth as an educator and a leader. Adam has had the pleasure of learning with and from John since he first stepped into a classroom, and he is forever grateful.

Adam's work as a consultant around comprehensive school reform focused on project-based learning and technology has afforded him many tremendous opportunities, but none are more valuable than the people he has met and learned from for all these years. Some of his mentors include Chris Corallo and Eric Jones in Henrico County, Virginia, and Mike Looney in Williamson County, Tennessee. Chris and Eric have been the driving force in Adam's growth as a leader and a consultant and have helped him develop the craft of asking the right questions and listening to learn. And while Mike and Adam haven't always seen eye to eye on education issues, Mike's abilities to craft a compelling argument and make others think have afforded Adam some of his best learning opportunities.

For both Bill and Adam, the staff of Solution Tree have been a tremendous support throughout the writing of *Teaching the iGeneration* and in the updated second edition that you now hold. Douglas Rife and Gretchen Knapp helped shepherd this book from an idea to a product that we are both proud of. Rachel Rosolina has served as our editor for both editions, taking rough drafts and turning them into much improved final copies with kind words every step of the way.

And while Adam and Bill don't have enough space to name every single superintendent, principal, teacher, or student that they have had the pleasure to work with over the past twenty years, both take a small piece of them everywhere that they go. It isn't very often that someone gets to say that they love what they do, but both Adam and Bill can. After all, they have been blessed to work with some of the most amazing educators and students in the United States. Those educators and students give both Adam and Bill hope that they can—and will—transform learning to meet the needs of the iGeneration.

Solution Tree Press would like to thank the following reviewers:

Steven Anderson
Instructional Technologist
Clemmons Middle School
Winston-Salem, North Carolina

Paul Cancellieri
Seventh-Grade Science Teacher
Durant Road Middle School
Raleigh, North Carolina

Howie DiBlasi
Technology and Educational Consultant
Digital Journey
Georgetown, Texas

Michael Fisher
Instructional Coach and Educational
   Consultant
Amherst, New York

Russ Goerend
Sixth-Grade Language Arts Teacher
Waukee Middle School
Waukee, Iowa

Kevin Jarrett
K–4 Computer Teacher and Technology
   Facilitator
Northfield Community School
Northfield, New Jersey

Meg Ormiston
Professional Development Specialist
Tech Teachers, Inc.
Burr Ridge, Illinois

Alan Veach
Principal
Bloomington New Tech High School
Bloomington, Indiana

Table of Contents

Reproducible pages are in italics.

Visit **go.solution-tree.com/technology** to download the reproducibles in this book.

About the Authors

William M. Ferriter—@plugusin on Twitter—is a sixth-grade science teacher in a professional learning community (PLC) near Raleigh, North Carolina. A National Board Certified Teacher, Bill has designed professional development courses for educators nationwide on topics ranging from establishing professional learning communities to integrating the Common Core State Standards into science and social studies classrooms. His educational technology training centers on using digital tools to give students the opportunity to drive meaningful change in the world around them. Bill has also developed schoolwide technology rubrics and surveys that identify student and staff digital proficiency at the building level. He is a founding member and senior fellow of the Collaboratory—a digital home for progressive conversations around the changing nature of teaching and learning—and has served as teacher in residence at the Center for Teaching Quality.

Bill has had articles published in *Phi Delta Kappan*, *Journal for Staff Development*, *Educational Leadership*, and *Threshold Magazine*. A contributing author to two assessment anthologies, *The Teacher as Assessment Leader* and *The Principal as Assessment Leader*, he is also coauthor of *Communicating and Connecting With Social Media*, *Building a Professional Learning Community at Work™*, and *Making Teamwork Meaningful*. Bill also maintains a popular blog—*The Tempered Radical* (blog.williamferriter.com)—where he writes regularly about teaching in today's world.

Bill earned a bachelor of science and master of science in elementary education from the State University of New York at Geneseo.

Adam Garry—@agarry22 on Twitter—is a former elementary school teacher and is now Dell's manager of global education strategy. He has presented at conferences around the world, including ISTE, and has delivered keynotes across the United States and in Costa Rica, Jamaica, and Trinidad. He has published many articles on technology integration for several education magazines and has a strong following on Twitter. Over the past twelve years he has consulted in school districts across the United States on school transformation, personalized learning, professional development, 21st century skills, technology integration, curriculum and instruction, and leadership. He was also one of the facilitators for the Partnership for 21st Century Skills professional development affiliates program and ISTE's School 2.0 workshops.

Adam received a bachelor's degree in elementary education from the University of South Florida, a master's degree in teaching and learning with a technology emphasis from Framingham State College, and a certificate in administration and supervision from Johns Hopkins University.

To book William M. Ferriter or Adam Garry for professional development, contact pd@solution-tree.com.

INTRODUCTION

The iGeneration

They have never known a life without the Internet, let alone computers, and many don't know a world without mobile phones.

—Sarah Cornish, *Total Girl* magazine

For most of the students gathered in the Davis Drive Middle School library in the late 1990s, school could not have been more exciting. Invited by NASA to participate in a global project, small groups of eighth-grade scientists were following the orbital path of the space shuttle *Discovery* as it traveled around the world. Because the space shuttle's onboard cameras could snap pictures of landforms on Earth, student experts were responsible for using the Internet—a relatively new tool for teachers and students at the time—to track world weather patterns, geographical features, and daylight hours.

When students realized that the space shuttle would be traveling over interesting areas of our planet—the Horn of Africa, the Strait of Gibraltar, the Black Sea, the Aleutian Islands—during daylight hours on a clear day, electricity would ripple through the media center regardless of the time. Students would quickly write up a photo request form and draft an email to NASA. If the request arrived in time—and if it was not buried under a pile of other requests made by different student groups scattered across the United States—the reward would be a digital copy of an orbital photo, something no student of the '70s had ever experienced.

For Dan—the teenage project manager selected by his peers because of his obvious passion for all things digital—the entire project was an experience in frustration. "I can't believe how slow these pages load!" he would shout at anyone who would listen. "If I was at home, I'd have this work done already, and we would have a better shot of getting our picture requests in on time. The Internet at school just plain stinks." No matter how hard his teachers worked to remind Dan that he was experiencing something new and unique—"*You are talking to the space shuttle, Dan. You couldn't have done that when I was in school."*—he was inconsolable. He was, after all, standing at the leading edge of the iGeneration.

Inheriting a world with nearly universal access to the Internet, iGeners—a term used throughout this text to describe the children of today's classrooms and tomorrow's workplaces—are almost universally plugged in. Ear buds hang from backpacks, and cell phones are stuffed into nearly every pocket. Text messages have replaced listening to voicemail, streaming video has replaced waiting for television shows to start, Xboxes and PlayStations have replaced Ataris, and high-speed wireless connections have replaced the dial-up modems that nearly pushed Dan over the edge. Even emailing NASA—so exciting in 1997—is considered tired and old-fashioned by iGeneration standards.

iGeners see technology as a tool for participating. They follow the lives of peers electronically, posting messages, videos, and pictures for one another in the latest social spaces. They join together to tackle video games with players from around the world. They rate everything from their teachers to their favorite songs. They use the Internet to organize around causes and take action together. Where their parents and teachers see the Internet as a place for gathering *information*, the iGeneration sees the Internet as a place for gathering *together* (boyd, 2008).

You know what the iGeners look like in your classrooms. They are willing to experiment their way through anything, confident that trial and error can crack the code better than reading manuals or following directions. They turn to the Internet first and the library second when assigned research projects. Their minds are working fast but not always as deeply or as accurately as the adults in their lives would like (Oblinger & Oblinger, 2005). "For young people," writes Derek Thompson (2014), "Facebook is the newspaper, and websites are the authors."

iGeners are also more emotionally open than anyone from previous generations. They are comfortable building relationships online, sharing the kind of information that makes their parents uncomfortable. They like working in teams better than working alone, and they use digital opportunities for interaction to try on new identities and personalities. For iGeners, technology is less important than the action that it enables. They are passionate about networking with others; digital tools simply make that passion possible (Oblinger & Oblinger, 2005). Often bored in school, iGeners spend their days texting under their desks, snapping pictures and videos with their cell phones, and (im)patiently waiting for the bell to ring so they can plug themselves back in.

The Dumbest Generation

For Dina Strasser, seventh-grade teacher and author of *The Line* (http://theline.edublogs.org), the technology-driven lives that students are leading carry costs that few educators or parents have ever really taken the time to consider. Students who are constantly connected end up disconnected, Dina argues, losing out on "real" experiences with other human beings or the environment around them. Local issues become irrelevant to teens who see the world as their audience. Ignoring diverse opinions is easy online.

"My worry is the fundamental concept of aloneness the Internet fosters," writes Dina, "disconnected not only from each other, but from our physical world. In terms of our *actual* human needs . . . the idea that we are, and can exist healthily, completely under our own steam is a pure falsehood. It's that simple" (D. Strasser, personal communication, March 30, 2008).

Tom Huston—the senior associate editor for *EnlightenNext* magazine—agrees, arguing that anyone under the age of thirty tends to swim in superficiality. He writes,

> Members of my generation lock and load our custom iTunes playlists, craft our Facebook profiles to self-satisfied perfection, and, armed with our gleefully ironic irreverence, bravely venture forth into life within glossy, opaque bubbles that reflect ourselves back to ourselves and safely protect us from jarring intrusions from the greater world beyond. (Huston, 2009)

Look closely at research around the screen and media behaviors of teenagers, and you will quickly realize that iGeners spend *most* of their lives inside of Huston's "glossy, opaque bubbles." In fact, the typical eight- to eighteen-year-old in the United States spends over seven hours a day *at home* behind a screen (Rideout, Foehr, & Roberts, 2010). "From the time I get home until I go to bed, I'm usually on my computer," reported fourteen-year-old Ben Knight in an interview with Masuma Ahuja (2013) of the *Washington Post*. What's more, constant connectedness is rapidly spreading beyond the home in a world where close to 40 percent of teens carry smartphones (Pew Research Center, 2012).

While connected, our kids surround themselves with content that can be difficult to admire. Despite having access to more educational media sources than previous generations—think the Discovery Channel and PBS Online—21st century teens are tuning in to *The Family Guy*, *Dance Moms*, *Pretty Little Liars*, and *The Vampire Diaries* (Kubicek, 2014). YouTube is their favorite web destination, and video games with mature content—Grand Theft Auto, Call of Duty, Assassin's Creed—are bestsellers (Downey, 2014; Thompson, 2014).

Social networking services like Facebook and Instagram have also become nearly ubiquitous among members of the iGeneration (Madden, 2013). With over half of all teens checking their social networking profiles more than once a day—and almost a quarter checking their profiles more than ten times a day—it is impossible to deny that virtual interactions are as important as face-to-face relationships for today's teens and tweens (Common Sense Media, 2009).

Academic Performance in the iGeneration

Another source of concern for parents and educators is the academic performance of the iGeneration. Despite living in a world of cutthroat global competition for knowledge-based work, U.S. students continue to underachieve in the classroom. As McKinsey & Company demonstrates in a review of Programme for International Student Assessment (PISA) results, the mathematical and scientific abilities of U.S. children lag behind students in countries that compete with the United States for high-value jobs. What's more, the gap between U.S. teens and their international peers only grows larger the longer they stay in school. "In other words," the report authors write, "American students are farthest behind just as they are about to enter higher education or the workforce" (McKinsey & Company, 2009, p. 8).

Results from the most recent National Assessment of Educational Progress reflect similar trends: only 26 percent of U.S. twelfth graders demonstrated proficiency in mathematics, and 38 percent of U.S. twelfth graders demonstrated proficiency in reading (National Center for Education Statistics, 2013). Knowledge of the core historical events and defining pieces of literature that have shaped thinking for generations is also waning. Less than half of our teens can place the Civil War in the proper century, almost 40 percent are unsure of when World War I happened, and nearly 30 percent don't know that Columbus sailed for America before 1750 (Hess, 2008). Perhaps we shouldn't be surprised, though, considering that only 40 percent of high school students report even being engaged in school (Busteed, 2013).

Statistics and trends like these led Mark Bauerlein—a professor of English at Emory University and one-time director of research and analysis at the National Endowment for the Arts—to declare the iGeneration the United States' dumbest generation:

> Whatever their other virtues, these minds know far too little, and they read and write and calculate and reflect way too poorly. However many hours they pass at the screen from age 11 to 25, however many blog comments they compose, intricate games they play, videos they create, personal profiles they craft, and gadgets they master, the transfer doesn't happen. The Web grows, and the young adult mind stalls. (Bauerlein, 2008, Kindle location 1683–1685)

Advancement of Learning

Bauerlein is particularly hard on teachers and other technology advocates, arguing that the millions of dollars districts have invested in digital tools to support learning have been largely ineffectual. Combating the view that schools should provide students with more time to explore and create online, Bauerlein (2008) writes:

> Ever optimistic, techno-cheerleaders view the digital learning experience through their own motivated eyes, and they picture something that doesn't yet exist: classrooms illuminating the wide, wide world, teachers becoming twenty-first-century techno-facilitators, and students at screens inspired to ponder, imagine, reflect, analyze, memorize, recite and create. (Kindle location 1900–1906)

And a closer look at the technology integration efforts in most schools might just reaffirm Bauerlein's doubts. While fewer than half of U.S. teachers believe that they can use technology to plan individualized lessons, almost 70 percent feel comfortable with using technology to complete administrative tasks, resulting in digital change efforts that achieve nothing more than "adding power to a marginal teaching approach" (National Education Association, 2008, p. 29).

Moving learning forward, then, begins by introducing teachers to ways in which digital tools can be used to encourage higher-order thinking and innovative instruction across the curriculum. iGeneration students, regardless of demographics, have shown an excitement for digital opportunities to learn, and technologists all over the world have created a range of tools that make collaboration, innovation, and individual exploration possible. Despite Bauerlein's skepticism, iGeners *can* be inspired by technology to ponder, imagine, reflect, analyze, memorize, recite, and create—but only after we build a bridge between what *they* know about new tools and what *we* know about efficient and effective learning.

A Focus on Verbs

For digital learning expert and author Marc Prensky (2009), building that instructional bridge requires a dedicated effort to separate nouns from verbs in conversations about teaching with technology. Verbs are the kinds of lifelong skills that teachers know matter: thinking critically, persuading peers, presenting information in an organized and convincing fashion. Nouns are the tools that students use to practice those skills. As Prensky (2009) writes:

> In teaching, our focus needs to be on the verbs, which don't change very much, and NOT on the nouns (i.e. the technologies) which change rapidly and which are only a means. For teachers to fixate on any particular noun as the "best" way (be it books or blogs, for example) is not good for our students, as new and better nouns will shortly emerge and will continue to emerge over the course of their lifetimes.
>
> Our teaching should instead focus on the verbs (i.e. skills) students need to master, making it clear to the students (and to the teachers) that there are many tools learners can use to practice and apply them.

A quick review of the literature around literacy and 21st century learning reveals—just as Prensky argues—that the popular verbs bear a striking resemblance to the essential skills that Benjamin Bloom described over fifty years ago. Will Richardson (2005), school change expert and author of *Why School?: How Education Must Change When Learning and Information Are Everywhere*, details one set of critical verbs in a 2008 post on his blog, where he writes,

> Our kids' futures will require them to be:
>
> - **Networked**—They will need an "outboard brain."
> - **More collaborative**—They are going to need to work closely with people to cocreate information.
> - **More globally aware**—Those collaborators may be anywhere in the world.
> - **Less dependent on paper**—Right now, we are still paper training our kids.
> - **More active**—In just about every sense of the word. Physically. Socially. Politically.
> - **Fluent in creating and consuming hypertext**—Basic reading and writing skills will not suffice.
> - **More connected**—To their communities, to their environments, to the world.
> - **Editors of information**—Something we should have been teaching them all along but is even more important now. (Richardson, 2008)

The Partnership for 21st Century Skills (2012)—an advocacy organization of business and education leaders brought together "to define a powerful vision for 21st century education and to ensure that students emerge from our schools with the skills needed to be effective citizens, workers, and leaders in the 21st century"—developed a similar set of skills in their often-cited *Framework for 21st Century Learning*. Along with a set of information, media, and technology skills, the framework describes three primary learning and innovation skills (Partnership for 21st Century Skills, 2009).

1. **Creativity and innovation:** The ability to generate, evaluate, revise, and act on original ideas, both as an individual and as a member of a collaborative group

2. **Critical thinking and problem solving:** The ability to make effective judgments based on evidence, to make connections between ideas, to reflect on learning experiences, and to evaluate potential solutions to critical issues

3. **Communication and collaboration:** The ability to articulate clearly, listen effectively, and select communication tools appropriately while making meaningful contributions to diverse groups

These skills are echoed in standards documents developed by national organizations representing teachers in nearly every content area. The Common Core State Standards (National Governors Association Center for Best Practices & Council of Chief State School Officers [NGA & CCSSO], 2010) lay out expectations that are designed to help students "reflexively demonstrate the cogent reasoning . . . that is essential to both private deliberation and responsible citizenship." The essential practices detailed by the Next Generation Science Standards (NGSS Lead States, 2013) include asking questions and engaging in evidence-based argument. The standards of the National Council for the Social Studies (2010) call for students to explore the ways that humans organize in order to promote positive societal change. Developing cross-cultural relationships to "pose and solve problems collaboratively" is encouraged by the National Council of Teachers of English (2013), and developing arguments and using reasoning to investigate are spotlighted by the National Council of Teachers of Mathematics (2004). Even the standards set by the National Association for Sport and Physical Education (2004) highlight higher-order verbs, requiring that students learn responsible behavior and respect for others during physical activities.

Following Prensky's advice by placing verbs first in instructional decision making, then, should make teaching and learning in a rapidly changing world more approachable for every teacher. Educators have spoken the language of higher-order thinking since our first pedagogy classes. We inherently recognize the difference between—and have a polished collection of strategies to support—experiences that require simple application of knowledge and those that ask students to synthesize information or to make judgments.

So rest assured. Instead of requiring a complete overhaul of the instructional practices in your classroom or building, moving learning forward in an increasingly complex world depends on nothing more than identifying the ways that new digital tools can facilitate authentic, student-centered experiences with the same enduring skills that you have been teaching for years.

How to Get Started

Much has changed since the first edition of *Teaching the iGeneration* was released in 2010. New sets of standards—including the Common Core Standards and the Next Generation Science Standards—have been released and adopted by states, redefining the work that happens in classrooms every day; new expectations for what students should know and be able to do before they graduate have been developed; and new tools and services have made learning even more efficient and effective for teachers and students. Our purpose for writing a second edition of *Teaching the iGeneration* was to refresh our text to take each of these changes into account. Our primary goal, however, remains the same: to help you to find the natural overlap between the work that you already believe in, the expectations that you are being held accountable for, and the kinds of digital tools that are defining learning in tomorrow's world.

Like the first edition of *Teaching the iGeneration*, each chapter of this text introduces one of five enduring skills necessary for success in any knowledge-based enterprise.

1. **Information fluency:** Intellectual discoveries rest at the heart of any true learning experience, which means that students must be able to systematically study content and question their own preconceived notions about the world around them. Questioning requires an ability to sort knowledge, identify sources of valuable information, and make frequent connections between ideas.

2. **Verbal persuasion:** In a world in which new content can be created and published easily, students should understand the strategies used to influence. They must be able to craft convincing arguments, recognize unsubstantiated claims, and find ways to raise their voices as individuals and as members of collective groups.

3. **Visual persuasion:** While verbal content will always be important, visual content is becoming increasingly significant when impacting audiences. Students must be able to organize images and videos in ways that draw their viewers in, choose fonts and colors that enhance rather than distract, and select media that deliver an emotional connection. They must also know how to dissect the media surrounding them in order to become more discerning and perceptive online.

4. **Collaborative dialogue:** Collective action, regardless of the circumstance, requires skilled communicators who can create meaning and work through conflict collaboratively. Students must be able to listen, summarize and draw conclusions, express positions, and see interactions with others as learning opportunities. Similarly, to succeed in knowledge-based workplaces, students must be able to appreciate alternative viewpoints, build consensus in the face of interpersonal conflict, and coordinate their efforts with other members of a team.

5. **Problem solving:** Our world is faced with a greater collection of borderless challenges than at any point in history. Drought, poverty, and global warming press nations to find international solutions to widespread problems. Our students must be able to operate within this

culture, constantly imagining, designing, implementing, and evaluating new approaches, regardless of the field in which they work.

Each chapter then details the digital solutions that can be used to enhance—rather than replace—traditional skill-based instructional practices. Readers will study the characteristics of different types of digital tools and explore teaching tips for overcoming common challenges associated with each tool.

A common thread you will find throughout *Teaching the iGeneration* is examples of students wrestling with global issues—the reasons that people hate one another, the struggles caused by poverty in the developing world, the impact that global warming and deforestation have had on the environment—regardless of the key skill that they are working to master. For educational change experts Michael Fullan and Will Richardson, challenge-centered projects like these are essential to developing the kinds of learning spaces that resonate with kids. For Fullan (2013), making progress on real-world issues is inherently motivating. "When you are engaged with others doing something meaningful," he writes, "you can accomplish wonders" (p. 70). And for Richardson (2012), the best classrooms are places where teachers create opportunities for students to "do work with others and make it work that matters" (Kindle location 280).

Another common thread that you will find throughout *Teaching the iGeneration* is references and connections to objectives from national and international organizations—the Common Core State Standards, the Next Generation Science Standards, the standards set forth by the International Society for Technology in Education, the standards detailed by the National Council of Teachers of English, and so on—that students will be wrestling with if their teachers implement the practices and activities outlined in each chapter. These references can be found at the end of each chapter in feature boxes titled "Curriculum Matters." They are intended to serve as a reminder that integrating challenge-based, skill-driven, technology-enhanced lessons does not mean ignoring the thoughts and ideas that currently govern our work. They are also designed to provide teachers with tangible reference points that they can use to explain their instructional choices to parents, principals, or policymakers who may not immediately see the benefits of reimagining classroom practices.

It is important to note that while the print version of *Teaching the iGeneration* includes dozens of handouts designed to support teachers working to use digital tools to help students master essential skills, you can visit bit.ly/TIGquickguide and plugusin.pbworks.com for an equally impressive and ever-changing collection of resources. On bit.ly/TIGquickguide, you will find a constantly updated list of tools and services that can be used to support the essential skills outlined in this book. On plugusin.pbworks.com, you can download additional lessons and explore examples of the kinds of meaningful work that students can tackle in a digitally connected classroom.

By extending the *Teaching the iGeneration* collection to the web, we are hoping to avoid the all-too-common pitfall of books focused on technology: content that ends up outdated as tools and services change over time. While readers must understand that some of the resources mentioned in this book will become obsolete, a quick visit to bit.ly/TIGquickguide or plugusin.pbworks.com should always connect readers to cutting-edge information about teaching and learning with digital tools.

Chapter Overviews

There is no one right way to read *Teaching the iGeneration*. Some readers will begin on page one and work their way straight through until the end. Others will identify an enduring skill, tool, or project that can be easily integrated into their current work. To help you decide on the strategy that is right for you, here is an overview of each of the five chapters.

Chapter 1: Managing Information in the 21st Century

In just a few short years, the way that researchers interact with content has fundamentally changed. A reliance on the Internet, in which a seemingly endless pile of sources awaits, has replaced our reliance on libraries and encyclopedias as homes for information. With nothing more than a few quick clicks, students can find everything from articles and research studies to blog entries, interviews, photos, and videos on nearly any topic. The challenge rests in sifting through this content quickly and reliably, identifying sources worth trusting, and eliminating sources that are not.

Chapter 2: Exploring Verbal Persuasion

Verbal persuasion has always been a skill that defined the most influential individuals in our society. Digital tools for publishing, however, make it possible for more people to be noticed—a new reality that hasn't gone unnoticed by governments. In a 2009 TED Talk, Gordon Brown—serving as the prime minister of the United Kingdom—argued that our wired world is allowing regular citizens to join together around ideas and to put pressure on their governments like never before (Brown, 2009).

Chapter 3: Exploring Visual Persuasion

While the text-based persuasive strategies introduced in chapter 2 are both essential and effective, visual content—still images and streaming video—has become an increasingly common tool for gaining influence in the world. Knowing that the iGeneration has been surrounded by visual messages for a lifetime, everyone from politicians and educators to corporate executives and army recruiters is working to use still images and video-based content to communicate messages. It is important to understand, however, that while the medium for communicating persuasive messages may have changed, the characteristics of the most influential ideas remain the same.

Chapter 4: Exploring Collaborative Dialogue

One of the most important lessons for teachers interested in integrating technology into their instruction is to meet students where they are. Learning experiences that incorporate the kinds of technology habits and behaviors that the iGeneration has already embraced beyond school are far more likely to generate high levels of enthusiasm, investment, and motivation. For most teachers, this means finding ways for students to use new media tools to communicate with one another.

Chapter 5: Exploring Collaborative Problem Solving

While evaluating information, elevating awareness, and attempting to influence thinking about controversial issues create many opportunities for meaningful learning experiences, productive global citizens must also be skilled at developing shared solutions to the challenges facing our planet. They must see value in crafting ideas together and in collecting multiple perspectives. They must be willing to open their own work to review and recognize that groups are inherently smarter than individuals when tackling particularly knotty issues. To put it simply, collaborative problem solving must be embraced in order for our world to survive.

We end the book with an appendix featuring a reproducible technology permission slip to inform all parents, teachers, and students about the rules and responsibilities of interacting online.

Final Thoughts

However you choose to tackle our text, remember that the purpose of *Teaching the iGeneration* is not to introduce you to new gadgets and gizmos. Instead, our goal is to help you find ways in which 21st century tools can support the kinds of experiences that encourage students to learn. As Peter Cookson (2009) explains, learning is a

> continuum of cognitive and expressive experiences that range from gathering data for the purpose of understanding the world; to organizing data into useful and coherent informational patterns; to applying information to real questions and problems and, in the process, creating knowledge; to developing wisdom that offers the hope of transcendent unity. (p. 8)

Reintroducing that sense of rigorous and systematic study to the iGeneration—a generation that has grown up connected but has failed to understand the power of connections—requires nothing more than a teacher who is willing to show students how the tools they have already embraced can make learning more efficient, more empowering, and more intellectually satisfying.

Are you ready to be that teacher?

CHAPTER **ONE**

Managing Information in the 21st Century

One key point often forgotten in conversations about teaching in a digital world is that the core instructional techniques of most classrooms remain unchanged. Students are still crafting written reports and position statements on topics of personal interest and global importance; powerful conversations still give students the opportunity to polish foundational beliefs; teachers still continue to expose students to the content of their curricula in the hopes of challenging preconceived notions; hands-on experiences are still an essential component of engaging classrooms; and information still stands at the center of meaningful learning experiences.

That's where the similarities between learning yesterday and today end, though. While the students of previous generations interacted with information by poking through card catalogs, manageable handfuls of books from the local library, or sets of encyclopedias purchased one volume at a time from the local grocery store, iGeners are surrounded by seas of online content. Considering that Google had indexed thirty trillion unique URLs on the Internet by March of 2013, it is easy to see how *too much* information can become a serious problem for iGeners (Koetsier, 2013).

To make matters worse, content posted online can suffer from the kinds of issues that traditional media sources—generally scrutinized carefully for reliability and quality before publication—have worked diligently to police. Websites can be outdated, contain inaccurate information, or be created by amateurs. Authors can attempt to influence their audience by posting biased information intentionally designed to deceive. While digital publishing has made content creation possible for more people, it has also removed the conventional barriers to publishing—high costs, trained writers, limited access to content—that have always served as reliability filters (Shirky, 2002).

Success in a digital world, then, requires students to be fluent with information. Before students can even begin to interact with content in a meaningful way, they must be able to search efficiently by picking out reliable sources and eliminating sites that stretch the truth. They must also be able to organize resources into collections that are easy to navigate and return to. Finally, they must be able to collaborate around research collections, taking advantage of the collective intelligence found whenever groups work together on information-based tasks (Surowiecki, 2004).

Luckily for learners, just as the volume of information available online has multiplied exponentially in the past decade, so has access to digital tools that can make managing information easy. The resources presented in this chapter are designed to introduce teachers and students to a handful of these tools—and to the core behaviors necessary for students to effectively navigate new digital landscapes. First, readers will learn about improved search engines that can help users break broad topics into sets of specific and manageable subcategories. Next, they will learn how to identify reliable websites, an essential skill for becoming a knowledgeable consumer of online content in a digital world. Finally, they will learn about content aggregators that automatically monitor sets of frequently updated websites and collaborative research tools that allow groups to build shared collections of resources and to have conversations around the ideas they are exploring together.

Surfing—and Searching—Efficiently

The first step in preparing students to pull together information in a media landscape dominated by digital content should always be to help students maintain focus in a world where they are surrounded by potential distractions. For Howard Rheingold (2012)—author of *Net Smart: How to Thrive Online*—maintaining focus is essential because losing focus carries costs:

> When you shift your attention, there is always a short interval during which you must reorient, refocus and filter out competing information in order to move from one stable theme to another . . . Cognitive scientists call this temporary disruption the attentional blink. Only you can tell whether shifting attention outside the boundaries of your focal theme is worth the time lost getting back to your original task ("switching costs")—but given experimental evidence, most people have to face that there *is* a cost, most of the time. (p. 39)

Rheingold goes on to argue that if we are going to survive and thrive online, we have to stop thinking about attention as something that is out of control. Instead, we need to take active steps—before, during, and after researching online—to create structure and discipline for our online selves (Rheingold, 2012). Teachers and students can use the handout titled "What Will You Click on Next?" (page 23) to provide this structure and to experiment with these steps.

After students have learned to maintain focus while working online, it is essential that they practice searching the web efficiently. While Internet searching may seem like a straightforward task, anyone working in classrooms knows that students approach web searches in a haphazard manner, jumping from link to link looking for information in a process that researchers Heather Horst, Becky Herr-Stephenson, and Laura Robinson (2010) call *fortuitous searching*. "Fortuitous searching represents a strategy for finding information and reading online that is different from the way kids are taught to research and review information in texts at school," write Horst et al. (2010):

> Students are taught to use tools such as identifying a purpose for reading, activating prior knowledge, predicting the content of a text before and during reading. . . . By contrast, fortuitous searching relies upon the intuition of the search engine and the predictive abilities of the reader. (p. 55)

While fortuitous searching may be a successful strategy for students exploring topics that they know well, it collapses whenever researchers lack the background knowledge that makes intuition and effective prediction possible. Young researchers studying new concepts enter generic terms—*volcanoes, World War II, famous mathematicians*—into search engines and are forced to sift through pages of websites unconnected to the topic of study or too sophisticated to understand. Inexperienced students also select topics that are too narrow for a research project—the average temperature of magma, the color of Allied uniforms during World War II, the birthplace of Pythagoras—and end up with limited content that cannot support an interesting and extensive final product.

The traditional solution to this challenge—and one that still works well—is to show students how to identify subcategories related to their research before turning to the web. Identifying subcategories can be done by generating lists of questions about a topic of study or by writing personal statements expressing individual reasons for pursuing a research project. Researchers can also focus on the chronologies, technologies, geographies, or biographies connected to particular themes—or even use the subheadings in common encyclopedias to set direction (Samuels, 2009). While methodically adding this kind of structure to research projects may seem to constrict the natural research practices of tweens and teens, we've seen firsthand that predetermined subcategories increase the likelihood that students will identify sources of value once they have started searching.

A digital solution to the challenge of focusing research efforts is to introduce your classes to instaGrok (www.instagrok.com). Designed specifically to break large concepts, events, and ideas into manageable groups of related subtopics, instaGrok can quickly point student researchers in new directions and help organize thinking around almost any issue. instaGrok can also adjust the complexity of search results based on the ability of student learners, return a list of related vocabulary terms for topics that are being studied, and automatically generate simple quizzes that can be used to test student mastery.

By instantly categorizing search results in an interactive web, instaGrok models the process that skilled researchers use to narrow topics and introduces students with little background knowledge to the key concepts connected to any subject. The handout "Searching With instaGrok" (page 25) included at the end of this chapter encourages students to use instaGrok to search for information, track the work that instaGrok does when sorting search results into subcategories, and reflect on instaGrok as a tool for facilitating research.

Rating the Reliability of Websites

While instaGrok can help students narrow topics and efficiently predict new directions for research projects, it offers no guarantees that the search results returned come from reliable sources. Just like researchers in any generation, your students must become adept at identifying the characteristics of sources that can't be trusted—and if the results of a study by the New Literacies Research Lab at the University of Connecticut (Krane, 2006) are any indication, this skill can be harder to master than you think. After introducing one of the Internet's most famous hoax websites (www.zapatopi.net/treeoctopus) to twenty-five seventh graders identified as accomplished online readers, researchers found that all but one believed the site was credible (Krane, 2006). In a related project in South Carolina, the New Literacies Research team found that nearly 60 percent of students surveyed report never bothering to check the accuracy of websites they are using for research (Bettelheim, 2007).

As intimidating as these numbers may seem, teaching your students to ask three questions while working online will leave them better prepared to identify reliable sources.

1. **Does the information on this website make sense?** The single best tool that researchers have for spotting sources that can't be trusted is their own common sense! Teach students to approach online content with healthy skepticism—and to find new sources whenever a site seems suspicious. With thousands of pages of content available online, there is never a good reason to settle on a source that contains questionable claims.

2. **What kinds of sources does this website link to?** Have you ever visually skimmed a Wikipedia entry? If you have, you've probably noticed that most entries include dozens of links. That's because responsible website authors understand that linking to sites containing proof of their claims earns respect and increases the credibility of their content. For student researchers, this means doubting sites that fail to provide readers with external sources to explore—or that link to sites that seem equally suspicious.

3. **Can I find any evidence of bias on this website?** Authors of sites studying controversial issues often have strong opinions about the topics that they are tackling. As a result, they tend to rely on emotionally loaded words and phrases that suggest unusual levels of urgency, passion, or action. While emotionally loaded words and phrases do not automatically mean that content is unreliable, they do suggest that an author is biased—and biased authors may intentionally fail to tell readers "the whole truth" about an issue.

These skills are introduced to students in the activity titled "Spotting Websites You Just Can't Trust" (page 27) and in the activity titled "Building a Collection of Web Sources" (page 28). In addition, the activity titled "Rubric for Scoring Your Collection of Web Sources" (page 30) can be used as a rubric by students who are evaluating sites that they are exploring for research projects.

Organizing Information

While independent searches will always play an important role in the study habits of digital learners, success in a world where thousands of pages of new content are posted daily and sites are changed almost hourly depends on a more proactive approach to information management. Success depends on the ability to fluently sift through digital noise. Content aggregators—also called feed readers—can help anyone consume online information more efficiently.

Feed readers are free, web-based applications that automatically check sites with frequently updated content. Users begin their work with feed readers by creating customized collections of interesting sites they would like to follow, a simple process that involves nothing more than copying and pasting web addresses into the appropriate menu bar of a content aggregator. Each time any of the sources in a user's customized collection changes, feed readers retrieve links to the new content, making it possible to instantly skim additions to dozens of websites in one place and at one time. For online consumers using feed readers, managing information goes from a frustrating search through thousands of sites to an efficient review of several trusted sources.

Classroom teachers are using content aggregators for three primary purposes, the first of which is to create resource collections for student researchers. Facilitating classroom research projects almost always begins by pointing students to sets of sources that are reliable. Feed readers, which often allow users to make their customized collections of sites publicly visible, can automate this process. Each time you begin a new unit of study, track down several current sources and organize them on a new page in a feed reader. By doing so, you can give students an online destination for constantly updated content covering the topic you are studying in class.

Second, teachers can use aggregators to monitor sites on which students are creating content or collaborating with one another. Ask teachers new to digital tools about their greatest fears, and you are likely to hear one answer time and again: "How am I supposed to monitor all of the content that my kids are creating? What happens if they post something inappropriate for the world to see?" Thankfully, feed readers make digital monitoring easy. Paste the web address for online projects—collaborative wikis, classroom blogs, asynchronous conversations between students—into your feed reader, and you will be notified every time new content is added by students.

Finally, teachers can use content aggregators to follow the thoughts and ideas of other teaching professionals. For classroom teachers, the most meaningful professional development opportunities begin and end with exposure to likeminded colleagues who are willing to make their practice transparent. While finding job-embedded time for this kind of collaborative reflection has always been a challenge, digital forums are breaking down the traditional barriers to learning in the schoolhouse (Ferriter, 2009). Each day, educators are connecting in online discussion groups or writing blogs that freely share resources and ideas with the world. If you are willing to invest a bit of time and effort into tracking down these conversations and organizing them into feed readers, you can create a differentiated tool for your own personal growth.

Like any digital application, there are literally dozens of feed reader programs to choose from, each with unique strengths and weaknesses. While it is impossible to predict which aggregators will remain popular and available over time, three have caught the attention of users. Many are drawn to the clean, advertisement-free layout of the pages provided by Netvibes (www.netvibes.com). Flipboard (https://flipboard.com) has become popular with users who consume the majority of their content on mobile devices like smartphones and iPads. Finally, Feedly (http://feedly.com) gives users the flexibility to set up news feeds in a variety of ways that range from simple lists to visually appealing tiles.

Educators and students have also been turning to Twitter to aggregate content from people all over the world. This content can be useful for the work they are doing in schools or for following an interest they have outside of work. Regardless, Twitter has become a main source of information for many people.

Collaborating Around Research

Learning to search the web efficiently, identify the characteristics of reliable websites, and use feed readers to organize information are largely independent tasks. And while they are essential skills for navigating a digital landscape, iGeners also need to learn to work collectively around research. That's where social bookmarking and shared annotation tools come in.

Social bookmarking and annotation tools allow groups of users to follow one another's web-based discoveries. For teachers willing to push the digital envelope, these tools can make collaborative research even more efficient and interesting for students. The challenge, however, is that social bookmarking and annotation are research practices that many students—and most teachers—have little experience with.

Social Bookmarking and Roles

In their simplest form, social bookmarking applications like Diigo (www.diigo.com) allow users to organize their own personal bookmarks in an online forum accessible from any computer connected to the Internet. When users share their bookmarks and tag collections with a group, however, their favorite resources become instantly available—and searchable—to anyone who cares to look. That means if your students are working with peers on a research project, they can see what their partners are reading related to their topic of study. Essentially, users of social bookmarking applications can help one another sift through the volumes of content available online. Rather than starting from Google, social bookmarking users narrow their focus by first exploring links their peers have bookmarked.

Like any collaborative school-based experience, successful social bookmarking projects depend on a teacher's ability to introduce productive group structures and behaviors. Clearly defining the tasks that students are expected to complete while working with one another helps reduce the kinds of frustrations that arise when students wrestle with new responsibilities and work patterns. Teachers who require students to brainstorm lists of common tags, create digital forums for communication, and set clear starting and ending dates for participation take the ambiguity that leads to friction out of social bookmarking projects.

Initial social bookmarking efforts also thrive when teachers assign specific roles to each member of student research groups. Specific roles assigned in advance serve as a tangible introduction to the kinds of unique practices that effective participants in social bookmarking communities engage in. They also ensure that the early efforts of student groups are successful, both in creating reliable collections of shared content and in learning to collaborate electronically, which builds classroom confidence. While the adult users of social bookmarking applications are unlikely to identify specific tasks for individual participants to complete, their behaviors generally fall into the same broad categories. Those categories can be introduced to students through the following six roles: (1) Original Thinkers, (2) Connectors, (3) Reliability Cops, (4) Mind Readers, (5) Johnny Opposites, and (6) the Cleaning Crew.

Original Thinkers

Any group of students working together with social bookmarking applications depends on having a healthy collection of web links worth exploring. The Original Thinker's role in a social bookmarking group is to bring content to the collective table by searching for websites connected to the current topic of study. While volume matters (Original Thinkers should plan to bookmark upwards of twenty sites for each research thread in order to ensure a measure of reliability in the information stream that a group studies), quality of content counts, too. Original Thinkers are essentially information filters for their partners. Careful selections can help groups make quick work of shared assignments.

Connectors

During the course of any research project, new strands of thought will naturally arise. The group studying Woodstock will want to learn more about acoustics. The group studying the Vietnam War will want to learn more about Cambodia. The group studying prime numbers will want to learn more about Euclid and ancient Greece. The Connector's role in a social bookmarking group is to be on the constant lookout for links related to these kinds of secondary themes. Without Connectors, social bookmarking groups will struggle to build the background knowledge necessary for understanding their primary topics.

Reliability Cops

While online resources have definitely made researching easier, they have also made researching riskier. That's because anyone can write anything online, whether or not it is true. Bogus websites filled with untrustworthy information can be found in any set of search results. That's where Reliability Cops come in. Reliability Cops must know everything there is to know about sniffing out websites that can't be trusted, and they must be willing to review every website that social bookmarking groups spotlight as worthy of continued study. Reliability Cops should delete any questionable sites from a group's shared collection.

Mind Readers

Some of the most valuable sources for finding new articles in social bookmarking applications are the libraries of public links automatically generated by other users. The Mind Reader's role in a social bookmarking group is to poke through these tag libraries looking for sites that may be valuable. Essentially, Mind Readers are looking into the collective brain of other users of social bookmarking services to tap into materials that their groups may have missed.

Johnny Opposites

Collections of web links built with social bookmarking tools are almost always susceptible to bias. After all, individual users make personal choices about the overall value of a site before adding it to a group's growing resources. Tackling controversial topics can result in one-sided studies. Deeply religious students may select different information to spotlight about natural selection and adaptation than students whose parents are university biology professors. Conservative students may select different information to spotlight about presidential elections than students who have recently joined the High School Democrats of America. The role of Johnny Opposites in social bookmarking groups is to make sure that personal biases don't taint a set of links by intentionally searching for sites that represent alternative viewpoints on any hot-button issue that their groups are exploring.

The Cleaning Crew

Social bookmarking efforts often collapse for one reason: group members get lazy and fail to annotate the shared links or to follow any kind of common tagging language. The result: haphazard collections of seemingly random web links that are no easier to explore than simple Google searches. That's where members of the Cleaning Crew come in. Understanding the important role that accurate titles, clean descriptions, and common tags play in efficient learning, the Cleaning Crew constantly reviews the bookmarks added to shared collections and polishes incomplete entries.

At the end of the chapter, we have included a checklist titled "Social Bookmarking as a Research Tool" that student research groups can use to guide their social bookmarking efforts (page 32); a note-taking guide titled "Social Bookmarking Roles" designed to introduce students to common roles in social bookmarking groups (page 34); and a handout titled "Building a Shared Collection of Bookmarks" that teachers can use to get several different classes to work together for a classroom research project on a controversial issue (page 36).

Shared Annotation

The shared annotation features of Diigo are even more motivating to students of the iGeneration—who are inherently social—than the social bookmarking features, because they make ongoing conversations around content possible. After installing a simple toolbar to their Internet browser, Diigo users can add highlights and text annotations to any web-based resource. For student research groups exploring content for classroom projects, this option provides a measure of targeted exploration between like-minded thinkers. Questions can be asked, thoughts can be challenged, and collective conclusions can be drawn quickly, easily, and transparently. No longer are novice researchers left to make sense of their studies alone. Instead, from any computer at any time, students can actively engage in a kind of "new reading" that adds real value to the research experience—a value that instructional expert Will Richardson (2009) believes will change the way that all of us interact with text:

> More and more I'm finding Diigo annotations and notes cropping up on the articles and essays that I read, and by and large I've found the commenters to be serious, thoughtful and articulate. . . . Those of us who are mucking around in these new reading and writing spaces have no formal training in it, obviously, just a passion to connect and a willingness to experiment and engage in conversations around the topics that interest us.

While there has been little effort to formally train students to work in new reading and writing spaces thus far, formal training can certainly help the shared annotation efforts in your classroom. Much like the structures suggested for social bookmarking projects, groups engaged in early attempts at shared annotation need clear tasks and timelines for their work. More importantly, students need training in the kinds of comments that add value to shared annotation projects. Specifically, teachers structuring successful shared annotation projects introduce three conversation behaviors to their students: (1) spotlighting key content, (2) responding to peers, and (3) asking questions.

Spotlighting Key Content

Shared annotation efforts depend on the ability of group members to identify content in online sources that will stimulate conversation. Group members who spot potentially valuable information must first highlight it and then add thoughtful annotations explaining the role that the content can play in a group's research efforts. Initial annotations must include sufficient detail to make a researcher's thinking clear and should be written using age-appropriate standards for grammar and spelling. To do otherwise makes communicating with digital group members inefficient and frustrating.

The pitfall for spotlighting key content in online annotation projects will resonate with any teacher who has taught note taking in their classrooms: students tend to add too many highlights, obscuring content that is truly valuable. To avoid this common trap, emphasize selective highlighting skills in your classroom. Require students to read an entire selection before adding any highlights. Then, encourage students to single out words and phrases rather than complete paragraphs of text. Finally, ask students to explain how the text they have chosen to highlight will benefit their group's research efforts (Santa, Havens, & Valdes, 2004).

Responding to Peers

Early efforts at shared annotation almost always reveal the same pattern: students add their own highlights and comments to a text but fail to read and respond to the thoughts of others. This is a natural pattern both for younger students who are not developmentally ready to think beyond themselves, and for older students who have inadvertently learned to act as individuals when it comes to schoolwork. It is also a pattern exacerbated by the novelty of new technologies. Students can be so excited about experimenting with digital tools that they overlook the content generated by other members of their research groups.

To avoid this trap, teachers must emphasize the important role that responses play in shared conversations around text. Start by encouraging students to read and react to the thoughts of their peers before adding new annotations or highlights to shared texts. Introduce the language of good responses by sharing simple sentence starters (*I wonder if . . . This reminds me of . . . This will be important to us when . . . I think this connects best to . . . I'm concerned that . . . I'm not sure I agree with . . .*) that can be used in conversations with classmates (Copeland, 2005). Model the kinds of comments that students can make when responding to peers by joining conversations around articles that research groups are studying. Shared annotation projects become truly productive only after students embrace the opportunity to react to the thinking of others.

Asking Questions

A third and final lesson that students tackling shared annotation projects must learn is that questions are the lifeblood of any learning experience. Without questions, good conversations simply die. That means almost every comment added to a shared text should end with a provocative question—or a series of questions—designed to elicit further conversation. Students can use questions to ask for specific feedback from group members, to push against the thinking of peers, to set new directions for research, or to clarify misunderstood positions.

Make questioning a more important part of your classroom's annotation efforts by celebrating the best questions added by peers to conversations. Create question banks for students to explore that include samples of the kinds of questions that continue conversations. Most importantly, model openness to being questioned by spotlighting instances in shared annotation efforts when students push back against your thinking. Practicing questioning skills will increase the depth and quality of the conversations that your students are having in shared annotation projects.

Shared Annotation Roles

Ensuring that these kinds of conversation behaviors become second nature in your classroom starts by assigning specific roles to members of student research groups working on shared readings for the first time. Rotating students through roles—and publicly spotlighting outstanding performances in class—can help guarantee that effective annotation habits take hold in your classroom. Five fun potential roles covering the kinds of behaviors essential to successful annotation efforts include Captain Cannonball, the Provocateur, the Middle Man, the Author's Worst Nightmare, and the Repo Man.

Captain Cannonball

Good conversations only begin with participants who are willing and able to find interesting ideas to talk about. That is Captain Cannonball's role in a shared annotation group. With a critical eye and an understanding of a group's interests and responsibilities, Captain Cannonball should find four or five key points in a shared reading to highlight and should craft initial questions for other readers to consider. Captain Cannonball's choices are important. The success of a shared reading often depends on the quality of the first comments and questions added.

The Provocateur

The best conversations always include a bit of passion. Disagreements, after all, are really nothing more than evidence of deep thinking, as participants work to defend, explain, revise, or refine their personal beliefs. Sadly, these opportunities for genuine learning are few and far between in school conversations because everyone plays nice, not wanting to make waves or to rock the boat. The Provocateur's role in a shared annotation group is to stir things up a bit, challenging the thinking of peers in the conversation. Directly responding to the comments made by others, the Provocateur reminds everyone that there are two sides to every story.

The Middle Man

Participants who are skilled at finding the common ground between different positions are just as important to successful conversations. Pointing out the overlap between two seemingly contradictory points of view helps all members of a group remain connected to one another and highlights areas for continued study. The Middle Man's role in a group annotation is to carefully consider the different perspectives being shared, looking for connections. The Middle Man often provides the glue that holds contentious conversations together.

The Author's Worst Nightmare

Shared annotation tools like Diigo allow groups to do something that was once unheard of: with a few digital clicks, users can challenge statements and ideas made by any author. No longer are readers required to simply accept that authors are experts who have the final word on topics being studied. Instead, readers can publicly push back against the assertions and ideas of authors.

That's the role of the Author's Worst Nightmare in a shared annotation group. Armed with a healthy dose of skepticism, the Author's Worst Nightmare questions statements made and conclusions drawn throughout a shared reading. While groups may eventually decide that an author's assertions are spot-on, the Author's Worst Nightmare's primary responsibility is to make sure that every point is considered carefully before it is accepted as fact.

The Repo Man

Shared conversations are only successful if groups walk away with a collection of shared ideas that can be used to focus future work. That's where the Repo Man comes in. The Repo Man's role in a shared annotation group is to carefully monitor conversations, looking for summary points that define exactly what it is that a group is learning together during the course of a collective reading. While the Repo Man's real work begins as a conversation is ending, he or she must stay in tune with the thoughts and ideas being shared as a conversation develops in order to identify important takeaways that a group can learn from.

An activity designed to encourage students to reflect on the characteristics of quality annotations (page 39), a checklist to guide student groups tackling shared annotation projects for the first time (page 41), and a rubric for scoring shared annotation efforts (page 43) are included at the end of this chapter to help you deliver shared annotation training to your students.

Final Thoughts

Since the 1990s, researchers have been attempting to describe a potential social crisis caused by inequitable access to new tools and technologies. According to this thinking, poor and minority communities would only fall further behind in a world working online. This *digital divide*—a term coined in the mid-1990s—exacerbated a condition that Pippa Norris (2001), the McGuire Lecturer in Comparative Politics at the John F. Kennedy School of Government, Harvard University, once described as "information poverty." She wrote:

> As the Internet evolved, a darker vision has been articulated among cyber-pessimists who regard digital technology as a Pandora's box, unleashing new inequalities of power and wealth, reinforcing deeper divisions between the information rich and poor, the tuned-in and the tuned-out, the activists and the disengaged. (p. 13)

The low cost of both computers and access to the web, however, have nearly eliminated this traditional view of the digital divide. Statistics collected from a 2014 Pew Internet and American Life Survey (Fox & Rainie, 2014) show that 87 percent of U.S. adults are actively using the Internet, including 68 percent who connect through mobile devices and tablet computers. A new digital divide, however, *is* developing between those using new tools and technologies to collect information and those who fail to move beyond traditional research and study practices. As *Edutopia* writer Richard Rapaport (2009) writes:

> Those stuck on the dark side of the new media digital divide will be as out of luck and out of touch as those who cursed Johannes Gutenberg as an agent of the devil when that first printed Bible came off the press in 1452. Gutenberg's invention offered a new, and to some, an intimidating, way of collecting, storing, disseminating, and even thinking about knowledge. More than five and a half centuries later, the rise of Web 2.0 and the new social media offers perhaps an even more profound method to expand the way people interact, communicate, and collectively create.

To put it simply, human patterns for interacting with ideas are changing dramatically. Making sure that your students end up on the right side of this new digital divide starts with intentional efforts to introduce the kinds of tools, strategies, and behaviors that make information management, fluency, and evaluation easy. Systematically teaching strategies for maintaining focus while online, searching the web efficiently, and identifying reliable content—as well as embracing content aggregation, social bookmarking, and shared annotation—will leave your students better prepared to succeed in a rapidly changing information landscape.

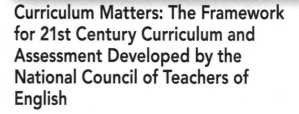

Curriculum Matters: The Framework for 21st Century Curriculum and Assessment Developed by the National Council of Teachers of English

For the National Council of Teachers of English (2013), literacy in the 21st century includes being able to "manage, analyze and synthesize multiple streams of simultaneous information." This means students should be able to find reliable information that meets their needs, analyze information from a variety of different sources, work individually and collectively around research projects, and identify digital tools that can support "communication, research and creation of new works" (National Council of Teachers of English, 2013).

Do these skills also appear in the curricula for your classes? Are they skills that you believe are important for iGeners? Which activities, strategies, and tools presented in this chapter would help students master these skills?

What Will You Click on Next?

Howard Rheingold—author of *Net Smart: How to Thrive Online*—argues that one of the most important skills to master is the ability to focus your attention while searching on the web (as cited in Barseghian, 2012). Rheingold suggests that learners should write down the three things that they want to get done *before* heading online. Then, they should make conscious choices about what to click on while surfing, only selecting sites that are likely to help them move toward their final goal. Use this handout to help guide *your* choices while working online today.

Questions to Answer Before Researching

1. **What three things are you hoping to accomplish while working on the web today?** If today were a perfect research day, what products or pieces of information would you walk away from the computer with?

2. **What kinds of resources or websites typically distract you while you are working online?** Do you catch yourself texting all the time? Checking your social sites? Playing online games?

3. **How are you going to avoid those distractions?** Would turning your phone off help? How about disabling notifications on your social sites?

Consider the following questions for each of the sites that you are thinking about exploring.

4. **What makes you think that this website is worth giving your limited time and attention to?** Which of your three daily goals do you think it will help you to accomplish?

5. **How long will you spend searching for information on this website before deciding to look elsewhere?** Does your confidence in the quality of this website change your plans for your remaining research time?

6. **What searching and sorting tools can you find on this website?** Is there a search bar? Are there category and/or topic links? Can you find lists of related resources?

Questions to Answer After Researching

1. **On a scale of one to five, how would you rate your productivity during today's research session?** Did you accomplish all of your key goals? Did you get distracted at all while researching? What caused you to lose focus?

2. **Which of the websites that you explored today were the most valuable?** Do these websites share anything in common? What can you be on the lookout for the next time you research to find more sites just like these?

3. **Which of the websites that you explored today were the least valuable?** Do these websites share anything in common? What can you be on the lookout for the next time you research to identify these websites early and avoid wasting time?

Source: Barseghian, T. (2012, August 31). What will you click on next? Focusing our attention online [Web log post]. Accessed at http://blogs.kqed.org/mindshift/2012/08/what-will-you-click-on-next-focusing-our -attention-online on October 21, 2014.

Searching With instaGrok

Often, the most challenging step in researching any topic is defining the most important subcategories—or strands of study—that broad ideas can be broken down into. But breaking broad topics into subcategories is really hard when that topic is new to you.

With instaGrok (www.instagrok.com) however, breaking a topic into subcategories and sifting through web-based resources is a breeze. Use this handout to identify a collection of categories and resources that may be worth exploring about the topic we are currently studying in class.

instaGrok Steps	Your Results
Begin by visiting instaGrok and searching for your broad topic the same way that you always have. instaGrok will automatically generate a web with your search term and a set of related subtopics. In the Your Results column, jot down the subtopics that seem the most interesting to you. Which ones will you explore?	Subtopics that you plan to explore:
Click the circle for one subcategory that you think is important to explore. instaGrok will automatically generate a new collection of subtopics worth exploring. In the Your Results column, jot down the subtopics that seem the most interesting to you. Which ones will you explore?	Additional subtopics worth exploring:
instaGrok also sorts resources into categories of content automatically: key facts, websites, videos, images, quizzes, glossary. Explore this content. Which category of content do you find the most helpful? Why?	The category of instaGrok content that I think is the most helpful is:

instaGrok Steps	Your Results
Perhaps the most important category of content that instaGrok returns are key facts. These short summary statements can provide you with quick background knowledge about the topic you are studying. If you click the More link at the end of each key fact, instaGrok will take you to a new web source that you can study. While researching, find a few key facts that you think are worth including in your report. Then, consider copying and pasting the web address for the sources that instaGrok points to. This will help you when you are finishing your research. Remember that you can use Bitly (http://bitly.com) to make long URLs shorter.	Key fact 1: Websites to explore: Key fact 2: Websites to explore: Key fact 3: Websites to explore:
One of the coolest features of instaGrok is that it will sort search results for you by difficulty. Experiment with this by clicking on the slider bar at the top of the screen. The closer the bar is to the ABC chalkboard, the easier the search results returned. The closer the bar is to the picture of Albert Einstein, the harder the search results returned. Is this helpful to you? Why?	Is instaGrok's difficulty sorting tool helpful to you as a researcher? Why? How? Which results were the most useful to you?

Spotting Websites You Just Can't Trust

To function effectively in our world, it is important that you understand that you can't automatically trust everything you find online. People use the Internet to share their opinions and to try to persuade readers to think a certain way.

As a researcher, it is your job to find facts and avoid being fooled by people who are not telling you the whole truth. This activity will help you judge the trustworthiness of a site that you are exploring by working through three key practices.

Lesson 1: Common Sense Matters

One of the best defenses against falling for half-truths told online is your own common sense. If something just doesn't sound right, you should automatically be suspicious!

Spend a few minutes working with a partner to gather statements from a website that you are skeptical about. Record your discoveries here.

Lesson 2: Look for Links

Knowing they must build readers' confidence, legitimate online content creators supply you with sources for the information they are sharing, and online readers should explore multiple sources before deciding what is worth believing.

Working with a partner, look for links on the website you chose in the previous lesson. Has the author included any? Are there any claims made in the text that you wish included links to sources or evidence? Does the author link to websites that you think are credible, or does the author link to websites that you have never heard of before?

Lesson 3: Look Out for Loaded Words

Whenever you are exploring websites about controversial topics, you are bound to come across words and phrases packed with emotion. These kinds of emotionally loaded words and phrases are a sign of bias. Authors who use loaded words and phrases have a strong opinion that they just can't hide—and that means they may intentionally present one side of an issue.

Working with a partner, read through the site that you are exploring. Do you see any loaded words or phrases? Are there places where the author lets his or her emotions about this issue show?

Building a Collection of Web Sources

Your job is to build a collection of web sources about a controversial topic we are studying in class. Use the checklist below to guide your decisions while building your collection. Remember that it is unlikely that every source will meet every criterion in the checklist—but the best sources and collections will definitely meet multiple criteria and the worst sources will only meet one or two criteria.

A Good Source Will	A Good Collection Will
Use statistics, star statements, and stories to support the author's point of view; strong opinions are those that are supported with convincing evidence. **Include links to other reliable websites** that discuss the issue in greater detail. **Avoid overly emotional words and phrases** even when the author is clearly taking a position in favor of or opposed to the controversial topic. **Highlight actual solutions to the controversial issue;** sources without solutions just aren't useful to readers. **Align with your common sense;** sites that seem too extreme or that just plain don't make sense don't belong in your collection. **Use proper grammar and spelling;** authors who can be trusted almost always take the time to proofread what they are writing. **Be written in age-appropriate language;** links that are impossible for your peers to understand aren't worth including in your collection.	**Include no fewer than eight and no more than ten sources;** too few resources means you haven't heard from enough voices, and too many sources can clutter your collection and overwhelm your audience. **Contain news sources that don't take any position on the topic** but instead share general information about the entire topic. **Spotlight sources that share a variety of perspectives** on the controversial topic—including people who are clearly in favor of and clearly opposed to the solutions being proposed. **Include a variety of sources**, including picture collections and videos. **Share the thinking of people**—individuals, companies, businesses, or colleges—that we have heard of before and we know we can trust. **Include current sources** as well as sources that show how the controversy has developed over time.

When you have found a useful source, be sure to write a three- to five-sentence description of why you have chosen to include it in our collection. Here's an example of what that might look like:

This source is useful because it explains several reasons why people should be opposed to the New York City soda ban without being overly emotional. The article comes from a health and fitness website, which surprised me because I thought they would be automatically in favor of the soda ban. The fact that they are opposed to it is convincing. I also like how the article includes a bunch of star statements from experts in health and fitness. That also makes it a convincing article.

Teaching the iGeneration © 2015 Solution Tree Press • solution-tree.com
Visit **go.solution-tree.com/technology** or **plugusin.pbworks.com** to download this page.

After you are done building your collection, answer the following reflection questions.

1. Which links in your collection do you think are the *most reliable*? Which do you think are the *least reliable*? Why?

2. Which links in your collection do you think will be the *most useful* to other people who are studying this controversial issue? Which do you think will be the *least useful*? Why?

3. Which links in your collection *reinforced, challenged,* or *completely changed* your initial thoughts about the controversial issue we are studying?

Rubric for Scoring Your Collection of Web Sources

Use the checklist and rubric below to evaluate your final web collection.

Questions to consider:

- **How reliable are the sources you have included in your collection?** Do they come from organizations or authors that you know and trust? Have you chosen any sources that you are unsure of? What makes you doubt those sources?

- **Do you include sources that are unbiased overviews in your collection?** Can people who know nothing about this topic easily find sources that will give them the background knowledge they need in order to better understand the issue we are studying?

- **Is your collection of sources balanced?** Did you include the same number of sources that are in favor of the issue we are studying as sources that are opposed to the issue? If not, which side of the issue is favored in your collection? Why did this imbalance happen?

- **Is your organization of sources logical and unbiased?** What have you done to make navigating your collection easier for the reader? Has the placement of sources been influenced at all by your own position on this issue? For example, if you are in favor of the issue, have you inadvertently sorted your collection in a way that favors sources that are also in favor of the issue?

- **Do you include a range of different source types in your collection?** Have you found pictures to include in your collection? Political cartoons? Videos? Charts and graphs? Or does your collection rely solely on text-based sources?

- **Are your sources age appropriate?** Who is the primary audience for your collection? Will they be engaged by the content that you have chosen to include in your collection? More importantly, will they be able to understand the content you have chosen to include in your collection? Are there any sources that are too difficult or too easy for your audience?

Scoring Rubric			
Criteria	**Beginning**	**Mastering** Student product includes evidence of all previous bullets AND	**Excelling** Student product includes evidence of all previous bullets AND
Quality of Content	Collection includes resources that are clearly connected to the topic we are studying.	Collection includes sources that almost always come from reliable authors or organizations. Both sides of the issue are represented equally in the collection.	There are no questionable resources in this collection. Placement of sources doesn't indicate bias of the collection's creator.
Level of Engagement	Readers could find something interesting to explore in this collection about both sides of the issue that we are studying.	Collection is organized in a way that will help readers understand both sides of the issue without difficulty. Collection includes age-appropriate resources.	Collection includes a nice variety of sources—images, video, text, charts, graphs. Readers will want to keep reading this collection.

Social Bookmarking as a Research Tool

One of the best ways for your research group to begin collecting and organizing information on the topic we are studying in class is to use a social bookmarking tool called Diigo (www.diigo.com). After your teacher creates student accounts for everyone in your class and introduces you to the basics of Diigo, use the following checklist to organize the work of your group.

1. Has your group brainstormed a list of common tags (keywords to organize your websites) that you will use when bookmarking websites for your research project? Does every group member have a copy of this tag list?

    Your Response / Next Steps:

2. Does your group have an Original Thinker who will bookmark at least twenty websites connected to your topic of study?

    Your Response / Next Steps:

3. Does your group have a Connector who will identify and bookmark resources on secondary topics? (Example: *Life expectancy is a secondary topic for poverty.*)

    Your Response / Next Steps:

4. Does your group have a Johnny Opposite who will ensure that the links you are collecting represent both sides of controversial topics?

    Your Response / Next Steps:

5. Does your group have a Reliability Cop who will rate the overall value of *every* web resource bookmarked based on how trustworthy it appears to be?

    Your Response / Next Steps:

6. Does your group have a Mind Reader who will dig through the Diigo bookmark lists (www.diigo.com/list/home) searching for sites that may be useful in your research project?

   Your Response / Next Steps:

7. Does your group have a Cleaning Crew who will ensure that every link in your shared collection has tags and short descriptions?

   Your Response / Next Steps:

8. Has your group worked out a plan for communicating during your initial efforts to identify and bookmark sites for your research project?

   Your Response / Next Steps:

9. Will you use the Topic option in Diigo? If so, has a new strand been posted already?

   Your Response / Next Steps:

10. Has your group set a starting date and an ending date for researching that everyone can agree to?

    Your Response / Next Steps:

Social Bookmarking Roles

Successful social bookmarking groups require participants to fill a range of roles. Use the following handout to take notes about the six social bookmarking roles and to assign tasks to each member of your social bookmarking team.

Role	Tasks
The Original Thinker	
The Connector	
The Reliability Cop	
Johnny Opposite	
The Mind Reader	
The Cleaning Crew	

Questions for Reflection

1. If you were to rank these social bookmarking roles in order of importance, what would your final list look like? Be sure to include a short explanation for each of your rankings.

2. Which of these social bookmarking roles do you think you would do well? Which of these social bookmarking roles would you likely struggle with? Why?

3. Make a list of your social bookmarking partners. Then, assign a social bookmarking role to each partner. Be sure to explain the character traits that will make your partners successful in the role that you've assigned to them.

Record your social bookmarking group assignments in the following table. Make sure that each group member has a copy of this handout and is aware of the role he or she is playing in your upcoming research project. There is room for a member's name, the role he or she will be taking on, and the reasons why he or she has been chosen for that role.

Member Name	Role Assigned	Explanation

Building a Shared Collection of Bookmarks

Today in class, we will use Diigo to build a shared collection of bookmarks that focus on the controversial issue that we are studying in class. Each class will have a different role to play in building our shared collection. Please find the directions for your class below.

Class 1: Bookmark sites that provide general information about the controversial issue that we are studying.

Your job is to search for *reliable* news sites that give a general overview of the controversial issue that we are studying. You should be on the lookout for sites that answer the basic questions that good news articles answer:

- **Who** is involved in this controversial issue?
- **What** are the important details that people need to know about this controversial issue?
- **Where** is this controversial issue taking place?
- **When** is this controversial issue taking place?
- **Why** were key decisions in this controversial issue made?

You should *not* bookmark websites that share too many opinions or that take a clear stand in favor of or against the controversial issue that we are studying.

In the comment section of your bookmark, please answer the following questions:

- What makes this article useful to readers? Is it written in language that other students will understand? Does it include an interesting video or graphics?
- What do you know about the author of the article? Why do you think we can trust what they are telling us?

Class 2: Bookmark sites that share reasons why the controversial issue is a *bad idea*.

Your job is to search for sources that explain why the controversial issue we are studying is a bad idea. The sites that you are looking for will definitely be sharing opinions—but remember that the best opinions are backed up by evidence.

While reading, be on the lookout for:

- **Statistics**—Evidence expressed in numbers or percentages
- **Star statements**—Quotes from experts (doctors, nurses, college professors, politicians, parents, store owners) who believe that the controversial issue is a bad idea
- **Stories**—The experiences of one individual with the controversial issue

In the comment section of your bookmark, please answer the following questions:

- What is the most convincing bit of evidence in this article? Why do you think that evidence is so convincing?
- What do you know about the author of the article? Why do you think we can trust what he or she is telling us?

- What do you know about the website that the article is posted on? Why do you think we can trust the content posted on this website?

Class 3: Bookmark sites that share reasons why the controversial issue is a *good idea*.

Your job is to search for sources that explain why the controversial issue we are studying is a good idea. The sites that you are looking for will definitely be sharing opinions—but remember that the best opinions are backed up by evidence.

While reading, be on the lookout for:

- **Statistics**—Evidence expressed in numbers or percentages
- **Star statements**—Quotes from experts (doctors, nurses, college professors, politicians, parents, store owners) who believe that the controversial issue is a good idea
- **Stories**—The experiences of one individual with the controversial issue

In the comment section of your bookmark, please answer the following questions:

- What is the most convincing bit of evidence in this article? Why do you think that evidence is so convincing?
- What do you know about the author of the article? Why do you think we can trust what he or she is telling us?
- What do you know about the website that the article is posted on? Why do you think we can trust the content posted on this website?

Class 4: Evaluate the bookmarks added to our shared collection by earlier classes.

Your job is to find an article that is already in our shared collection and determine (1) whether it is worthwhile and (2) whether it is believable.

While judging whether your article is worthwhile, ask yourself the following questions:

- Will other students find this article easy to read, or is it written for older readers? Why?
- Is this article easy on the eyes? Are there graphics (videos or pictures) to look at? Are the paragraphs short, or are they really long? If another middle schooler lands on this page, will he want to read on or will he be too intimidated by what the page looks like to want to read any further?
- Does this article have links to other articles about the controversial issue that we are studying that readers can explore?

While judging whether your article is believable, ask yourself the following questions:

- Does the author of this article share enough evidence in the article to make a strong case or does it seem like the author is doing nothing more than sharing his or her opinion without backing it up with supporting details?
- Does the author of this article seem like an expert that is worth trusting? Is there enough information about the author and about the website that the article appears on to make them believable?

- Is there anything about this article, this author, or this website that seems suspicious or that makes you skeptical? What (if anything) do you doubt about this article, this author, or this website?

After exploring your website, please add a comment in our classroom group that answers the following questions:

- On a scale of 1 to 5 where 1 is the worst and 5 is the best, how worthwhile is the website that you were evaluating? Explain the reasons behind your rating.

- On a scale of 1 to 5 where 1 is the worst and 5 is the best, how believable is the website that you were evaluating? Explain the reasons behind your rating.

- Would you recommend this article to a friend who wanted to learn more about the controversial issue that we are studying? Why, or why not?

Reflecting on Diigo Annotations

One of the keys to really taking advantage of Diigo (www.diigo.com) as a student research tool is learning to make quality contributions to the conversations that your peers are having around articles. Use this handout—which includes a strand of conversation between sixth-grade students—to reflect on the characteristics of quality annotations and Diigo conversations. This strand addressed a current event article about a U.S. company's work in Peru.

Original Text Highlight: U.S.-owned Doe Run Corporation bought the smelter from the state in 1997 on the condition that it would reduce toxic emissions.

Comments Added to Highlight

- Interesting—this is another example of a U.S. company owning a factory in South America. Remember that South American countries often have natural resources but they don't have the tools to do anything with those natural resources, so companies from countries like ours come in to do the work. So the question is, should we feel bad about the fact that a U.S. company is polluting heavily in Peru? (comment by William Ferriter)

- I think that we should feel bad for the fact that we're putting other children at risk so we can earn more money. Just because those children are not our children, doesn't mean we shouldn't care about their health. Also, these factories emit lead into the air. So do you think it's ok for the U.S. to ban lead in our country, but then go and buy a factory that basically pumps lead into other children? Do you think it's fair that we're shortening these children's lives so our country can get more money? (comment by Caroline W.)

- Caroline said: *Do you think it's fair that we're shortening these children's lives so our country can get more money?* Absolutely not! We have enough money already. As one of the wealthier countries in the world, we don't have the right to bully the underdeveloped countries. We should be helping them not hurting them. If we want to make world peace, helping underdeveloped countries is a good start. The poor countries tend to fight more because they are in major need of money, natural resources, land, or something other than that. We also don't want the poor Peruvians to get mad at us. On the flip side, we are in an economic crisis. Do you think that the people leading the business need money or want to provide jobs? I still don't think that matters as much as helping out other countries. What do you think about this situation? (comment by Anna E.)

- I think the people who lead the business don't really care about the health of the people in Peru, near the smelter. They probably only care that they get money from the job that it provides. If they did care, they wouldn't even be over there pumping lead into the air and peoples' bodies. The U.S. banned this for a reason: it was harming the peoples' health who live around it. For us to go over there and do it to the people of Peru just isn't right. We already know what it does to our health, and we don't care. Do you think the extra money for the U.S. is worth harming other peoples' health? (comment by Kristen W.)

Questions for Reflection

1. What do you notice about each of these comments? Are there any shared strengths to the comments? Shared weaknesses? What impresses you? What turns you off?

2. What kinds of things do each of the participants in this conversation do to encourage their peers to share their thoughts? How important do you think that is for groups reflecting on articles together?

3. Which comment in this strand of conversation adds the most value to the thinking and work of the group? Why?

Shared Annotation Checklist

Once your group has started a healthy collection of websites to explore for your research project, you can use the shared annotation features of Diigo (www.diigo.com) to take notes and wrestle with key ideas together. After your teacher has introduced social bookmarking and shared annotation to you, use the following checklist to organize and evaluate your shared annotation efforts.

1. Has your group used the social bookmarking feature of Diigo to create a healthy collection of websites to explore together?

    Your Response / Next Steps:

2. Does your group have a Captain Cannonball, whose job it will be to craft initial comments and add initial highlights to your collection of shared websites?

    Your Response / Next Steps:

3. Does your group have a Provocateur, whose job it will be to challenge the thinking of his or her peers in shared annotation conversations?

    Your Response / Next Steps:

4. Does your group have a Middle Man, whose job it will be to find common ground and to draw conclusions based on the range of statements made in a shared annotation conversation?

    Your Response / Next Steps:

5. Does your group have an Author's Worst Nightmare, whose job it will be to challenge statements and ideas made by the authors of your articles?

    Your Response / Next Steps:

Teaching the iGeneration © 2010, 2015 Solution Tree Press • solution-tree.com
Visit **go.solution-tree.com/technology** or **plugusin.pbworks.com** to download this page.

6. Does your group have a Repo Man whose job it will be to create a list of summary statements at the end of a shared annotation conversation?

   Your Response / Next Steps:

7. Do all of the comments in your shared conversation use proper annotation language? Are they proofread carefully? Do they begin with lead statements and end with questions? Do they demonstrate deep thinking? Do they add value to your studies?

   Your Response / Next Steps:

8. Have you created a plan for deleting highlights or annotations that are throwaways? How will you hold your peers accountable for posting quality thoughts to your conversation? For fulfilling their role in your shared annotation group?

   Your Response / Next Steps:

9. Has your group set a starting date and an ending date for commenting that everyone can agree to?

   Your Response / Next Steps:

Scoring Shared Annotation Efforts

Improving shared annotation efforts requires regularly reviewing the content that groups are creating together. Students and teachers alike can use the following rubric to judge the quality of the work done around any shared reading.

Above Average
▪ The highlighting on this shared reading draws attention to ideas that are essential for this group's research efforts. There is no evidence of excessive highlighting or of decisions to spotlight unimportant information.
▪ This group does a great job using annotations to carry on a conversation with one another. Questions are asked and answered, ideas are raised and challenged, and new thinking is generated together.
▪ I'm impressed because the researchers used proper grammar and spelling in all situations, making it easy to understand their ideas. There weren't any places where I struggled to understand what annotations meant.
▪ Overall, this shared annotation project was amazing! I learned a ton just by reading through the thoughts shared by the members of this group.

Average
▪ While this group has definitely highlighted valuable information, in places it was hard for me to sift through all of the highlights to figure out what exactly was important.
▪ Many of the annotations in this shared reading seem like first drafts to me. They include enough information to catch my attention but not enough information to really make me think.
▪ I see a lot of people doing a great job making their own thinking clear, but there are not many questions being asked or answered between members of this group.
▪ I had no trouble understanding the writing in any of the annotations added by researchers. Students used proper grammar and spelling in almost every situation—which meant that I knew exactly what they were trying to say.
▪ Overall, this shared annotation effort left me interested but wanting to know more.

Needs Improvement
▪ I was left guessing by a lot of the highlights on this reading. Adding annotations to explain the reasons that pieces of content were highlighted would have helped me.
▪ There were lots of playful interactions between members of this research group in the annotations that weren't related to the topic of the article.
▪ There wasn't a lot of meaningful interaction between group members in the annotations on this article. I would have loved to see them asking and answering questions with one another.
▪ There were a lot of spelling and grammar errors in the annotations around this article that made it difficult to understand just what the student researchers were trying to say.
▪ Overall, this shared annotation effort left me wanting more.

Teaching the iGeneration © 2010, 2015 Solution Tree Press • solution-tree.com
Visit **go.solution-tree.com/technology** or **plugusin.pbworks.com** to download this page.

Questions for Reflection

If you had to defend the score that you have given this group, what evidence from their highlights and annotations would you use? Can you find any specific highlights and annotations that support your final rating?

Which individual members of this student research group made the most meaningful contributions to their team's efforts? What was it about their contributions that were impressive to you?

What specific suggestions for improvement would you make to the members of this student research group? How can they improve their shared annotation efforts?

Teaching the iGeneration © 2010, 2015 Solution Tree Press • solution-tree.com
Visit **go.solution-tree.com/technology** or **plugusin.pbworks.com** to download this page.

CHAPTER TWO

Exploring Verbal Persuasion

One of the most powerful opportunities afforded by our new media environment is the chance to be heard. While the students of earlier generations felt just as passionately about controversial issues as the students who currently sit in our classrooms, iGeners can use digital tools to easily join together to raise and amplify their voices, gaining a level of influence and awareness equal to (or even greater than) the influence and awareness held by adults.

The challenge is that students are not automatically prepared to be any more influential than peers from earlier generations. While they may have access to tools that allow them to be heard, being heard is only valuable when the messages shared are worth listening to. In a world in which anyone connected to the web has instant access to millions of perspectives, thinkers who do a poor job differentiating their ideas and articulating compelling points of view remain powerless.

As a result, the initial resources presented in this chapter have little to do with technology. Instead, we begin by exploring materials designed to introduce students to the traditional practices that authors use to sway readers. We introduce the characteristics of convincing evidence and share examples of persuasive writing, laying a foundation for effective argument that can translate across any genre for communication. We also provide handouts that can be used to track and evaluate the proof collected for persuasive pieces. Working through these materials can help ensure that your students understand the role that reliable evidence plays in developing credibility.

Only then will we investigate one of the most approachable digital tools for elevating student voice around controversial issues: blogs. We will explore a series of structures, handouts, and suggestions designed to ensure that classroom blogging efforts are successful. Then, we introduce you to *#SUGARKILLS* (http://sugarkills.us), an effort on the part of author Bill Ferriter's sixth-grade students to persuade teens that there is too much sugar in the food they are eating on a daily basis.

Understanding Verbal Persuasion

One of the most articulate advocates for verbal persuasion is Don Rothman, senior lecturer emeritus at the University of California, Santa Cruz. Rothman has spent the past thirty years teaching students how writing can be used as a tool for public discourse and civic engagement. "I have come to see quite vividly literacy's potential to enhance democracy," argues Rothman, "especially around the intellectual and social practices that make nonviolent persuasion possible. Literacy, of course, doesn't guarantee freedom of expression, but writing, in particular, offers opportunities for people to counter alienation, isolation, and selfishness that undermine democracy" (as cited in Brown, 2005, p. 43).

In an interview with Dan Brown—editor of the *Higher Education Exchange*—Rothman describes three key factors successful written persuasion depends on (Brown, 2005).

1. **A respect for other people's views:** Persuasion, argues Rothman, is often misinterpreted as bad manners, primarily because of a resistance on the part of public figures to acknowledge how their own beliefs have been shaped by the thoughts, ideas, and opinions of others. Making room in persuasive arguments to show an appreciation for diverse viewpoints can earn influence and allies. Convincing others to embrace novel ideas requires a willingness to highlight the natural connections between their core beliefs and new directions.

2. **A willingness to sustain conversations:** The most effective arguments are built only after careful listening. Meaningful conversations between individuals who disagree can result in a collective intelligence around controversies. Silencing opponents—inadvertently or intentionally—only leads to underinformed positions, and underinformed positions are rarely persuasive. That means writers who learn to sustain the thinking of others are in a better position to understand complex issues.

3. **An ability to accurately, and civilly, describe sources of disagreement:** Divergent ideas are inevitable in persuasive conversations, and the approach that thinkers take when addressing disagreement often determines how influential they will be. While modern culture celebrates aggressive responses designed to humiliate perceived "opponents," effective persuasion depends on the ability to disagree agreeably. "It means being able to describe quite accurately what you disagree with," writes Rothman, "presenting respectfully the logic of a misguided argument" (as cited in Brown, 2005, p. 48).

Like many of the skills presented in this book, iGeners are unlikely to embrace Rothman's key points without regular instruction. While the traits of effective written persuasion can definitely be learned, they are rarely modeled by public figures. To ensure that your students reflect on multiple perspectives while wrestling with important issues, introduce the "Recognizing Different Perspectives" handout found on page 53. Then, use the "Collecting and Respecting Different Perspectives" handout (page 54) to structure meaningful conversations between students with divergent viewpoints. Finally, the "Exploring Misguided Arguments" handout (page 56) can help students craft thoughtful responses to people holding on to faulty core beliefs.

Distinguishing the Characteristics of Convincing Evidence

While successful persuasive projects should begin by developing a clear understanding of opposing viewpoints, thinkers must eventually craft independent positions. Scaffolding this process starts by sharing the characteristics of convincing evidence with novice learners. Three approachable evidence categories that can be introduced to the students in your classroom are (1) statistics, (2) star statements, and (3) stories.

Statistics

Statistics are facts or pieces of information expressed as a number or a percentage. Statistics are some of the most convincing bits of evidence in persuasive pieces because they make abstract concepts concrete and tangible. What's more, statistics allow readers to make simple comparisons between new topics and their own lives. Finally, statistics can be presented visually in charts and graphs—and visual representations of abstract concepts can be interesting and easier to understand.

Star Statements

Star statements are direct quotes from experts, eyewitnesses, world leaders, and/or popular celebrities. Star statements lend credibility to persuasive pieces, proving to readers that an author's core beliefs are recognized and respected by outside authorities. Star statements also add a sense of voice to written pieces. The most effective persuaders, however, carefully select statements from the kinds of stars admired by their target audiences. While the thoughts and opinions of elected officials are likely to carry weight with adults, statements from athletes, celebrities, or musicians would be more convincing in pieces designed to persuade teens.

Stories

Stories share direct experiences with the topic being studied. Like statistics, they provide concrete examples of the impact that abstract concepts have on individuals and/or communities. What's more, stories are teaching tools that every reader has experienced. "People change how they view the world through the telling of vibrant and credible stories," write Kerry Patterson, Joseph Grenny, David Maxfield, Ron McMillan, and Al Switzler (2008, p. 61). While finding credible stories about controversial topics can sometimes be challenging for novice writers, the efforts invested almost always result in written pieces that are far more persuasive.

At the end of this chapter, you will find three handouts designed to introduce the characteristics of convincing evidence to your students. The first, "Evaluating Persuasive Letters" (page 57), allows students to rate two persuasive letters written by middle grade students. The second, "Convincing Evidence Tracking Sheet" (page 58), can be used by students to ensure that their persuasive pieces include a nice balance of statistics, star statements, and stories. Finally, the "Persuasive Writing Scoring Rubric" (page 60) can be used to give students feedback on persuasive projects.

Structuring Classroom Blogging Projects

Once your students are comfortable with the characteristics of written persuasion, they will finally be ready to share their personal opinions with a larger audience—and there isn't a more popular tool for sharing opinions than blogs, one of the original Web 2.0 tools. With millions of authors posting new content to the web each day, blogs have been embraced as a nearly universal tool for reaching audiences.

Blogs are popular because they make web-based publishing easy. No longer do users have to understand complicated computer programming languages to post their ideas online. Instead, they can simply choose from a range of free blogging services, create an account, and begin writing! The windows and toolbars that users see after signing in to blogging services look identical to the windows and toolbars of most popular word processing programs. Icons for changing the color and size of text are paired with icons for inserting pictures, bulleted lists, and web links. Users can even tag posts—much like websites can be tagged in the social bookmarking applications introduced in chapter 1—to create categories for their writing. After entries have been polished, publishing to the web is a one-click process that opens student ideas to a broader audience than they have ever had the opportunity to write for previously.

Classroom blogging projects require a measure of structure before they will be successful, however. Before creating a digital home for your students' efforts at verbal persuasion, consider the following school-based blogging tips and tricks.

Posting All Content on One Cause-Driven Classroom Blog

One of the first questions that teachers ask when starting classroom blogging projects is, "Should I have each student in my class create his or her own blog?" The answer is a resounding no! For blogs to survive and thrive, they need a constantly updated stream of content. Because most K–12 students will struggle to generate content consistently over a long period of time—and because monitoring the content posted on dozens of individual student blogs can be an overwhelming challenge for any teacher—it is best to start classroom blogging with one blog that every student in your class can post to.

To give your students opportunities to practice verbal persuasion, consider centering your blog on an individual cause or controversy that motivates your students. Whether they are working to draw attention to poverty and injustice in the world, trying to address a national environmental challenge, or creating a tool for informing and educating friends and neighbors about issues affecting your local community, your students will be far more motivated to write for your classroom blog when they feel like they are tackling a topic that is meaningful and important to their audience.

Encouraging Students to Become Regular Readers of and Commenters on Others' Blogs

Believing that blogs are *only* opportunities for students to practice writing skills is a fatal flaw for most classroom blogging projects. Instead of digital soapboxes, teachers and students must begin to see blogs as interactive forums for continuing conversations around topics of interest—and interactive forums require two-way participation. That means your students need to become avid readers of and commenters on blogs, too. Consider organizing a collection of student blogs in a public feed reader that your students can visit during silent reading time or while surfing the web at home.

Encouraging students to read blogs written by other students serves three primary purposes. First, students who read blogs are likely to see models of persuasive writing that can be used as models for their own work. Second, students who read blogs are likely to be exposed to ideas for interesting topics they may want to explore in new entries of their own. Finally, students who read blogs connect with potential audiences.

As your students begin reading blog entries, you should systematically teach the skills necessary for writing effective blog comments because comments give students opportunities to practice reacting to ideas in writing. What's more, comments left on entries written by other authors can serve as first drafts for future posts on your classroom's blog. Finally, commenting emphasizes the community nature of blogging and draws reciprocal readers—people interested in looking closer at the ideas expressed by your students—to your classroom's blog. The handout "Leaving Good Blog Comments" (page 61) can be used to introduce your students to the language of blog commenting.

Tracking down age-appropriate blogs that are of interest to your students often starts at the Comments4Kids website and hashtag (http://comments4kids.blogspot.com; http://bit.ly /comments4kidshashtag). Both are digital projects maintained by William Chamberlain (@wmchamberlain) that are designed to raise awareness of student blogging projects. Teachers interested in finding long-term blogging partners to collaborate with may also be interested in exploring Quadblogging (http://quadblogging.com), a project that pairs four classes together for regular cycles of reading and commenting on one another's blogs.

Promoting Student Blog Entries to Parents and Colleagues

While writing for the web ensures that your students will eventually have readers from every corner of the globe, the vast majority of your blog's readers—and almost all of your commenters— are going to be your students' parents, the students of your colleagues, and educators that you have made connections with in faraway locations, because parents, colleagues, and students in classrooms just like yours have a stake in the learning your students are doing online. That is what makes them willing to read what your kids are writing and to leave a comment every now and then.

As a result, work hard to *promote* your students' writings with parents and colleagues. Send out links to pieces that you are particularly proud of or that are likely to stimulate exciting conversations. Ask parent volunteers to stop by once a week and leave feedback for students who have posted new entries. Not only do students need feedback in order to remain motivated by your classroom blogging efforts, but feedback from those who matter—moms, dads, teachers, and best friends—is far more meaningful than the occasional comment left by an outsider, regardless of where he or she is from.

Naming and Training Student Editors

Teachers who are starting classroom blogging projects often enthusiastically jump in with two feet, encouraging classes to churn out dozens of entries, promoting posts with parents and peers, and building new lessons with their blogs in mind. Then, they end up buried by entries that are poorly written or by students who need technical help posting new pieces. Eventually, they begin to question whether the time they are investing in monitoring student work and in facilitating digital novices is really worth it.

That's why student editors are so important for successful classroom blogging projects. Training a handful of super-motivated students to proofread new entries and to support students struggling with technical skills can ensure that teachers don't suffer from "monitoring burnout." Over time, you will have veteran student editors who take great pride in the blog that your class is producing. Not only will they continue to write for you once they have left your class, but they will also serve as competent gatekeepers, polishing entries that are not quite ready to be published, monitoring comments that are being posted, and generating enthusiasm for the work that you are doing online.

Regularly Exploring Visitor Maps and Page View Statistics

As motivating as local readers can be for student bloggers, discovering that visitors from all over the world stop by to read their work never fails to amaze tweens and teens. To prove to your students that their efforts to persuade are reaching readers in faraway locations, be sure to include a visitor map in the sidebar of your blog.

While there are many services that will track the location of the visitors that land on your site, ClustrMaps (www.clustrmaps.com) is one of the most popular because it highlights each visitor with a red dot on a digital image of the world. Before long, red dots will cover entire continents, reinforcing the idea that your students are being heard! ClustrMaps also reports the number of page views that your website receives on a regular basis—and can break those page view statistics down by continent. Consider asking students to track this information carefully in their notebooks or on a classroom bulletin board. Watching your readership grow over time will be just as motivating to your students as seeing where their readers are coming from.

On page 64, you can find a checklist designed to help teachers think through the technical and pedagogical preparations that go into successful classroom blogging projects; on page 67 you can find a scoring checklist for student blog entries; and on page 69 you can find an overview of three popular blogging platforms that are worth exploring.

Persuading Teens to Think Twice About Sugar

In the spring of 2013, the students in Bill Ferriter's sixth-grade science classroom were studying the efforts of New York City Mayor Michael Bloomberg to ban the sale of sugary drinks in containers larger than sixteen ounces (Lerner, 2012). In the course of their studies, Bill's students began to look carefully at the amount of sugar in the foods that teens and tweens like to eat. What they found shocked them: while doctors recommend that teens and tweens eat no more than twenty-four grams of added sugar *in one day*, foods popular in the middle school cafeteria—fruit snacks, flavored drinks, frosted donuts—often included more than twenty-four grams of added sugar *in one serving*. Even yogurt—a seemingly healthy lunch option that many students ate on a regular basis—had an unhealthy amount of added sugar in each cup.

Bill's students decided to start blogging about the amount of added sugar in foods in an attempt to persuade their peers to make better choices while eating. To date, their blog—*#SUGARKILLS* (http://sugarkills.us)—has had over 25,000 views and 140 comments from over 100 countries around the world. Every day, Bill's students post new bits that include a simple graphic comparing the amount of sugar in popular foods to doctor recommendations, along with a short written piece designed to reach young readers. And every day, visitors land on *#SUGARKILLS* after searching Google for information about the amount of added sugar in foods. Each visit, page view, comment, and post serves as tangible evidence that Bill's students have a voice—and as they explained in a 2013 interview with *MiddleWeb* magazine, having a voice matters:

> Our goal for *#SUGARKILLS* was simply to inform people about the sugar in the foods they commonly eat and to help people make better choices. That has been a success from the beginning, and we're proud of that. But what makes us even more proud is that we have helped people all around the world with their sugar intake.
>
> A couple weeks ago, Mrs. Swanson left us a comment about how her dad has diabetes and our blog is really helping him. It makes us feel great to know that we have made a difference in someone's life. What if Mrs. Swanson's father made the decision to say "no" to one candy bar, because of us? Then he would keep making healthier choices, and that could eventually save his life! We have made a huge difference.
>
> We have also discovered that other teachers are actually sharing our work with their students, which makes us feel like we really matter to other people. How many 12 year old students can say that they are changing people's lives around the world? The fact that we can is amazing! (MiddleWeb, 2013)

The lesson for classroom teachers is a simple one: teaching students to be verbally persuasive can and should start with attempts to write publicly for real audiences on topics that matter—a process made possible by blogging.

Final Thoughts

For many teachers, classroom blogging projects are a risky move they are unwilling to take because they lack faith in the quality of work that their students can produce. As Mike—a high school English teacher and regular reader of *The Tempered Radical* blog (http://blog.williamferriter .com)—explained in the comment section of a 2007 blog post:

> I'm usually amused, but more dismayed when a colleague informs me that they've just dis-covered the Internet . . . and blogging software and plan to use it to transform the lives of their students. I'm dismayed because what they commonly end up doing is wasting huge amounts of class time as their students write poorly, with little evident reasoning, in a medium that exposes their lack of ability to a much wider audience. (Mike, 2007)

Classroom blogging efforts are only a huge waste of class time when they are poorly struc-tured or when students are forced to write about topics that they have little passion for. "Nobody can be forced to do this," write Charlene Li and Josh Bernoff (2008), authors of *Groundswell* and experts on the use of social media tools to drive change. "Blogging is too personal, and requires too much effort, to be crammed down anybody's throat" (Kindle location 1208–1211).

To avoid the same pitfalls, focus first on the kinds of content likely to leave your students jazzed—in this case, persuasive pieces centered on controversial topics related to your curricu-lum. Then, help students collect, evaluate, and collaborate around information connected to their topic of study. Finally, explore samples of effective writing and the characteristics of con-vincing evidence. Only then will your students be ready to produce the kind of content you can be proud of.

Curriculum Matters: The Common Core State Standards

Students wrestling with the Common Core State Standards are expected to develop argu-ments that are supported with "clear reasons and relevant evidence" (NGA & CCSSO, 2010). This means students should be able to identify accurate and credible sources to reinforce their core beliefs; to use varied evidence types includ-ing quotations, examples, facts, and details effectively when working to be influential; and to fairly address any claims and counterclaims that readers are likely to have in persuasive pieces (NGA & CCSSO, 2010).

Do these skills also appear in the curricula for your classes? Are they skills that you believe are important for iGeners? Which activities, strategies, and tools presented in this chapter would help students master these skills?

Recognizing Different Perspectives

One of the keys to being persuasive is the ability to understand the full range of perspectives that people may hold on the issue you are studying. Before crafting the final copy of your persuasive piece, use this handout to think through how others may feel about the same topic. Responses can be built on student predictions, conversations with peers, or evidence collected while researching.

Questions to Consider	Your Response
How do you feel about the controversial topic we are studying?	
How would people who are completely opposed to your point of view feel about the controversial topic we are studying?	
Is it possible for people to mostly disagree with your point of view but see at least something positive in your positions? How would they feel about the controversial topic we are studying?	
Is it possible for people to mostly agree with your point of view but see some weaknesses in your positions? How would they feel about the controversial topic we are studying?	

Collecting and Respecting Different Perspectives

Now that you have thought through a range of different perspectives about the controversial issue we are studying in class, it is time to seek out real voices from real people who disagree with you. Engaging in conversations with those who think differently will help you understand the issue you are studying better. Use this handout to collect viewpoints that don't align with your own.

Conversation Planning Steps

Who do you intend to speak to? (This can be any classmate, family member, or friend who you know thinks differently than you do.)

When do you plan to speak to this person? (Do you have time to meet during the school day? Is there a due date that you must be aware of? How will you get in touch with this person?)

How do you expect this person to feel about the controversial issue you are studying? (Is he or she likely to completely disagree with your point of view? Will there be any common ground between your perspectives?)

Is there anything about this person's age or experiences that might shape the way he or she thinks about the topic you are studying? (Is he or she likely to have firsthand experience with the topic you are studying? Will experience—or inexperience—influence his or her point of view? Will age, family background, or hometown influence his or her point of view? How?)

What questions do you most want to ask this person? How will you challenge his or her thinking? What do you most want to understand? (The best conversations are built on questions! If you want to encourage other people to talk, you have to concentrate on asking and listening instead of talking and telling. Brainstorming good questions now will help you sustain conversations later.)

Taking Notes During Your Conversation

What key points does this person make about the issue that you are studying? (Are there ideas that he or she repeats time and again? Does he or she use phrases like, "What I really believe . . ." or "Most importantly . . . ?")

What kinds of attitudes or emotions does this person display during your conversation? (Does he or she seem open to new ideas? Is he or she angry? Excited? Emotional? How does he or she respond to challenges that you pose? Which ideas fire him or her up? Which ideas do he or she seem the least interested in?)

How does this person answer the questions that you ask? (Remember that you came into this conversation hoping to understand new perspectives. Record as many details as you can.)

Reflecting on Your Conversation

What new ideas did you learn about your topic during this conversation? (Careful thinkers can *always* learn something new from people who have different points of view. What caught your attention during this conversation? What points caught you by surprise? What hadn't you considered before?)

What new ideas did you learn about your opponents during this conversation? (Are there specific points that they feel particularly strongly about? Are there specific points they might be convinced to change their mind about? What kinds of language do they use?)

Are there parts of this person's point of view that resonate with you? What is impossible for you to agree with? (Persuasion often depends on finding common ground between different points of view. Where is the overlap between your thinking and the positions of this person? What are the flaws in his or her thinking? How can you respectfully convince this person that his or her ideas are flawed?)

Note: While speaking with an actual person will be far more meaningful, it is not required to gather different perspectives. You can also search the Internet to collect multiple viewpoints on the issues you are studying.

Exploring Misguided Arguments

There are times when you will be involved in conversations with well-intentioned people who are inadvertently sharing inaccurate information. While they may passionately believe that they have shaped their positions carefully, there are flaws in their thinking. The best persuaders can accurately describe the sources for disagreements and respectfully point out misguided arguments. Use this handout to structure your responses to individuals who hold inaccurate ideas about the topic you are studying.

What core belief do these people hold that you think is flawed? (Be as specific as possible when describing their point of view. Include statements that they have made or facts that they have used to defend their point of view.)

Why would a reasonable person think this way? (What is it about the flawed point of view that would resonate with reasonable people?)

Are there any public figures who agree with this flawed point of view? If so, what kinds of messages are they sending to listeners? (Use the Internet to track down any comments being made by public figures—politicians, musicians, sports stars—that might influence the way people think about the topic you are studying.)

Specifically, what is wrong with the core belief you are questioning? What evidence can you provide to prove that this core belief is flawed? (Questioning the emotions and personalities of the people you disagree with is unproductive. Instead, stick to the facts. What is it that you think your opponents have failed to think through carefully? What clear and convincing evidence can you provide to call their flawed thinking into question?)

Note: Remember that your opponents feel as strongly about their core beliefs as you feel about yours. Effectively challenging flawed thinking often means finding the admirable qualities in their position. Doing so makes it clear that you don't doubt their intentions or competence.

Evaluating Persuasive Letters

Convincing evidence can make all of the difference when you are trying to be persuasive. Need proof? Then check out the following two sample letters designed to convince President Barack Obama to take action on global poverty, and answer the reflection questions found at the bottom of this page.

Persuasive Letter 1

Dear President Obama,

Imagine if you had grown up in the same Angolan town as Jonas, a twelve-year-old boy who is struggling to survive even as we speak. You see, his country is being destroyed by a civil war that has been raging for nearly twenty-five years.

For Jonas, that means a lack of clean water and safe shelter. It means that schools are rarely open and that his father has spent more time away from home fighting than he has with his son. It means fear and hunger and, most of all, poverty.

If you were Jonas, your life expectancy would be thirty-seven years—barely old enough to even run for president here in the U.S.—and there would be a 40 percent chance that you couldn't even read or write.

Is helping people who live in poverty the kind of change you were talking about when you were elected, Mr. Obama?

Jonas hopes so . . . and so do I.

Persuasive Letter 2

Dear President Obama,

Do you realize how lucky you were to be born in the United States of America? After all, you could have been born in a million different countries on a million different continents, and there's not a single place that would have been better than here.

Think about it. What would your life be like if you were born somewhere else? Would you be the president? Probably not. Would you be able to read? Probably not.

You probably wouldn't even have food to eat or a roof over your head. You certainly wouldn't have the fancy homes and cars that you have now.

That's why you should care about poverty. I do.

Questions for Reflection

1. If you were to rate the two persuasive letters on a scale of 1 to 5—with five representing the highest score possible—what scores would you give? Why?

2. Working with a partner, identify and provide an example of each of the different types of convincing evidence—statistics, star statements, and stories—used in persuasive letter 1. Circle the piece of evidence used in persuasive letter 1 that you think is the most convincing.

3. Working with a partner, list three places in persuasive letter 2 where the author could have inserted a statistic, star statement, or story. Explain what type of evidence you would have tried to find had you written this piece.

Convincing Evidence Tracking Sheet

Now that you have had the chance to evaluate two persuasive letters, it is your turn to begin collecting convincing evidence for the persuasive piece you will write. Use this handout to begin organizing the convincing evidence that you find while you are researching. In the first column, write the evidence you plan to include in your persuasive piece. Be accurate with numbers and names. In the second column, select the type of evidence you are collecting. Tracking the types of evidence used will ensure your piece is interesting to readers. In the last column, include the title, author, and page number of your source. If the source is a website, use www.bit.ly to shorten the address.

Evidence	Type	Source
	❑ Statistic ❑ Star Statement ❑ Story	
	❑ Statistic ❑ Star Statement ❑ Story	
	❑ Statistic ❑ Star Statement ❑ Story	
	❑ Statistic ❑ Star Statement ❑ Story	
	❑ Statistic ❑ Star Statement ❑ Story	
	❑ Statistic ❑ Star Statement ❑ Story	

page 1 of 2

Tasks for Reflection

Now that you have finished collecting a set of convincing statistics, star statements, and stories, spend a few minutes completing the following reflective tasks:

1. **Rank your evidence** in order from the most convincing to the least convincing. Explain your thinking.

2. **Generate a list of evidence** that you would still love to find. What statistics, star statements, or stories would make your persuasive piece even more convincing?

3. **Rank your list of sources** in order from the most valuable to the least valuable. Which sources should you return to first if you need to find more convincing evidence to add to your persuasive piece? Why?

4. **Have a peer or a partner check your ranked lists.** Does he or she agree with you? Why, or why not?

Teaching the iGeneration © 2010, 2015 Solution Tree Press • solution-tree.com
Visit **go.solution-tree.com/technology** or **plugusin.pbworks.com** to download this page.

Persuasive Writing Scoring Rubric

Parents, students, and teachers can use the following rubric to rate persuasive pieces created by students.

Above Average
<ul><li>You have definitely taken a stand on the issue we are studying—and you have supported your position with really convincing points.</li><li>You have addressed all of the "complaints" that opponents are likely to have with your point of view, detailing the flaws in their thinking or leaving readers convinced to move forward anyway.</li><li>I'm impressed by the evidence that you have found to persuade your readers. You have done a great job balancing statistics, star statements, and stories in your piece.</li><li>Your writing is top-notch. It is clear and easy to understand, with no spelling or grammar errors. Your paragraphs are all approachable—none are too long and none are too short—and your use of varied sentence lengths, figurative language, and interesting vocabulary makes your piece fun to read.</li><li>Overall, your piece changed the way I feel about this issue.</li></ul>

Average
<ul><li>You have definitely taken a stand on the issue we are studying—and more importantly, you have supported your position with several good points.</li><li>In places, you have done a good job using convincing evidence—statistics, star statements, and stories—to persuade your readers. In other places, though, you make statements that are not backed up with evidence. While the reader might be able to guess why the points you are making matter, the best persuaders never make their readers fill in the blanks.</li><li>While there is nothing particularly fancy about your sentence structure or vocabulary, there are few mechanical errors in your piece that are going to leave your readers confused.</li><li>Overall, your piece convinced me that this issue mattered and that your point of view makes sense.</li></ul>

Needs Improvement
<ul><li>I'm not sure I know what your point of view is on the issue we are studying in class. I struggled to follow your thinking, and I'll bet that other readers will struggle, too.</li><li>I'm also not sure that you have chosen the most convincing evidence for your piece. While you have included a few statistics, star statements, and stories, they don't always seem connected to the topic we are studying.</li><li>Some of my biggest struggles were caused by grammar and spelling mistakes. At times, understanding your writing was difficult.</li><li>Overall, your piece didn't leave me convinced that this issue mattered.</li></ul>

Leaving Good Blog Comments

The best blogs are truly interactive, with users listening and responding to one another. They are interesting digital conversations! Highly accomplished commenters are constantly thinking while interacting with others who are leaving comments. They come to the conversation with an open mind, willing to reconsider their own positions—and willing to challenge the positions of others. The following tips will help you craft great blog comments.

Gather Your Thoughts

To be an active blog commenter, start by carefully reading the original post. Then, take the following steps while working your way through the comments left by others.

Tasks	Your Response
Gather facts. Jot down things that are interesting and new to you. Facts often become the source for fascinating questions or new strands of conversation.	
Make connections. Relate and compare things you are hearing to things you already know from your personal life or your studies.	
Ask questions. What confuses you about the comments that have already been made? What don't you understand? Remember that there will *always* be questions in an active thinker's mind.	
Give opinions. Make judgments about what you are viewing and hearing. Do you agree? Do you disagree? Like? Dislike? Do you support or oppose anything that you have heard or seen? Why?	

Source: Tasks adapted from Santa, C. M., Havens, L. T., & Valdes, B. J. (2004). Project CRISS: Creating independence through student-owned strategies (3rd ed.). Dubuque, IA: Kendall/Hunt.

Craft Your Comment

Good blog comments require the same skills as any piece of writing—careful proofreading, solid elaboration, and accurate punctuation. Use the following steps to craft a good blog comment.

Task	Your Response
Include an opening quote. While commenting, try to respond directly to other readers. Begin by quoting some part of the comment that you are responding to. That will help other readers know what has caught your attention. Example: Jack K. posed a wonderful question: "Do adults hate more than children do?"	
Elaborate—even if you don't agree. Next, explain your own thinking in a few short sentences. Elaboration is important when you are trying to make a point. When responding to another reader, don't be afraid to disagree with something he or she has said. Challenging another reader will help him or her reconsider his or her own thinking—and will force you to explain yours! Just be sure to disagree agreeably; impolite people are rarely influential. Example: Chyna argued that adults are more likely to hate than children. I agree with her mostly because adults have had more experiences with people than children have. When you haven't had many experiences, you are less likely to jump to conclusions about others—and often, hate starts when we jump to conclusions about people that we disagree with.	
Answer questions. Point out places where you are confused. Raise perspectives that haven't been considered. Make comparisons to topics that you've already studied. Share what surprises you—either about the topic or the thoughts of your peers. Example: I think that we all hate the same but the hate starts with parents, teachers, and others in authority. It's really hard not to adapt to what everyone else is thinking or doing. Hate is a strong feeling toward a certain person because he or she is different—and we all know people who are different.	

Teaching the iGeneration © 2010, 2015 Solution Tree Press • solution-tree.com
Visit **go.solution-tree.com/technology** or **plugusin.pbworks.com** to download this page.

Task	Your Response
Finish with a question. Digital conversations are like any good conversation—they depend on interesting questions and new strands of thought to keep them alive. That means the best blog comments end with a question designed to keep people talking. Your question should be open ended, which means participants shouldn't be able to respond with a yes or no answer. It should also be related to the body of your comment. Finally, it should be interesting enough to make others want to respond! Example: That idea poses another question for me: Do you think that people who hate are afraid of difference or are they really just afraid of change? Isn't it more comfortable to stay the way we are than to try to become something new?	
Prepare to be challenged. If another reader challenges your thinking in a blog conversation, don't be offended. Listen to your peers, consider their positions, and decide whether or not you agree with them. You might discover that they've got good ideas you hadn't thought about. Either way, respond—let your challengers know how their ideas have influenced you.	

General Reminders

Don't ever use your real name or the name of your school when commenting! Remaining anonymous is the safest way to add comments to blogs.

Don't respond to anyone who says something inappropriate to you in a blog comment. Find your teacher if this happens!

Be sure to proofread your posts carefully. Tons of errors will make people think that you don't know what you are talking about.

Teaching the iGeneration © 2010, 2015 Solution Tree Press • solution-tree.com
Visit **go.solution-tree.com/technology** or **plugusin.pbworks.com** to download this page.

Teacher Checklist for Blogging Projects

Because blogging projects mirror work that most teachers are already having students do in class—producing written content—they are a natural first step for digital novices. The following yes or no questions will help you determine whether or not you are prepared to facilitate blogging projects in your classroom. Under "Your Response / Next Steps," list what needs to be done along with a date for when this action should be completed.

Technical and Procedural Preparations

1. Does your school or district's technology services department have a preferred blogging service? Have they already made arrangements for students or teachers to have free accounts at those services?

    Your Response / Next Steps:

2. Have you checked with your school or district's technology services specialists to learn more about any restrictions they have placed on the creation of digital work by students?

    Your Response / Next Steps:

3. Are you aware of any Internet safety policies or procedures in place at the school or district level that may influence your blogging project?

    Your Response / Next Steps:

4. Have you informed parents that their children will be maintaining an online forum for reflection? Are you planning on asking parents to sign a permission slip before students can participate in your blogging project?

    Your Response / Next Steps:

5. Have you made a decision about whether to create one classroom blog or individual blogs for each of the students in your class or on your team?

    Your Response / Next Steps:

6. Are you planning on using a feed reader (content aggregator) to organize a collection of blogs for your students to read and respond to?

    Your Response / Next Steps:

7. Have you developed a comfort level with the basic steps involved in crafting and posting entries in the blog service that you plan to use?

    Your Response / Next Steps:

8. Are you planning on using visitor map and stat tracker services like ClustrMaps (www. clustrmaps.com)?

    Your Response / Next Steps:

Pedagogical Preparations

1. Have you thought through the kinds of entries you would like to see students making on your classroom blog?

    Your Response / Next Steps:

2. Do your students understand the important role that links play in blog entries? Are they capable of identifying reliable sites to include as sources in their blog posts?

    Your Response / Next Steps:

3. Do your students understand the important role that commenting can play in student blogging projects?

    Your Response / Next Steps:

4. Have you considered training a small cadre of student technology leaders to serve as student editors? Do these editors have a clear sense of their responsibilities? Will there be any rewards for filling this role?

    Your Response / Next Steps:

5. Are you planning on advertising student blog entries with the parents of your students and your professional colleagues in order to drive traffic to your site?

    Your Response / Next Steps:

6. Have you worked with your students to set realistic and measurable goals—number of posts, number of comments, number of page views, visitors from foreign countries—for your classroom blogging project?

    Your Response / Next Steps:

Teaching the iGeneration © 2010, 2015 Solution Tree Press • solution-tree.com
Visit **go.solution-tree.com/technology** or **plugusin.pbworks.com** to download this page.

Blog Entry Scoring Checklist

As your class begins to craft blog entries connected to controversial issues or classroom content, you can use this checklist to evaluate blogging assignments.

Questions to Consider

1. Has the author tackled a topic that is interesting or appropriate for his or her intended audience? Does the topic connect to something being studied in class? To a broad theme running across content areas?

   Your Response / Next Steps:

2. Is there evidence that the author has thought deeply about the topic of study? Are you convinced that he or she is clearly and transparently wrestling with new ideas here?

   Your Response / Next Steps:

3. If the author is tackling a controversial issue, has he or she expressed his or her position in an articulate, convincing, and responsible manner?

   Your Response / Next Steps:

4. Has the author used statistics, quotations, anecdotes, and stories effectively to express his or her point of view? Are readers likely to be influenced by this post?

   Your Response / Next Steps:

5. Has the author included extensive links to reliable outside sites designed to provide readers with evidence for central claims or sources for continued study?

   Your Response / Next Steps:

page 1 of 2

6. Has the author used age-appropriate grammar and mechanics? Has the piece been carefully proofread to ensure that mistakes don't interfere with the reader's understanding?

   Your Response / Next Steps:

7. Does the author spark conversations with readers by asking provocative questions or expressing interesting positions in this post?

   Your Response / Next Steps:

8. Will readers want to respond to this blog entry? Can they work in new directions, generating posts that build from the strands of conversation introduced by this author?

   Your Response / Next Steps:

9. As comments are added to this entry, has the author worked to continue the conversation by responding to readers? Do his or her responses ask questions, challenge thinking, or demonstrate a willingness to be challenged?

   Your Response / Next Steps:

10. Will readers walk away from this blog post and ongoing comment conversation knowing more about the topic being studied?

    Your Response / Next Steps:

Final Thoughts

What makes you proud about this blog entry? How can this author improve his or her final product?

Popular Blogging Platforms

While it is impossible to predict which blogging platforms will remain popular with teachers and authors, three tools have stood the test of time.

1. **WordPress** (www.wordpress.com): WordPress is one of the most popular blogging services used both in and beyond schools. It is known for clean themes and layouts, which authors enjoy and appreciate. It also gives students experience with a tool that is widely used beyond school for publishing.

2. **Blogger** (www.blogger.com/features): Blogger is Google's blog service, which makes it another tool that is worth introducing to students who are likely to spend their lives working with Google's products. While Blogger has many of the same features of WordPress, the visual layout of Blogger blogs is not as polished or interesting.

3. **Kidblog** (http://kidblog.org/home): Kidblog is a blog service that is specifically recommended by and for elementary school teachers. One of the primary advantages of a service tailored for younger students is that you can find sample blogs worth exploring. Kidblog also provides student accounts and safety features that are customized for individual age groups.

CHAPTER **THREE**

Exploring Visual Persuasion

The minds behind VitalSmarts have spent the past thirty years helping Fortune 500 companies make the kinds of rapid behavioral changes that result in growth. Drawing from their experiences as leaders of nonprofit organizations, researchers studying management theory, and consultants charged with improving team dynamics, Patterson et al. (2008) combined their collective experiences to coauthor *Influencer: The Power to Change Anything*—a title that examines just what it takes to be persuasive.

In *Influencer*, the VitalSmarts team argues that the key to being persuasive is a teaching tool as old as time: well-told stories. Stories provide listeners with opportunities to work through imaginative rehearsals, seeing situations through the eyes of participants instead of simply attempting to understand as outsiders. What's more, stories appeal to human emotions—and human emotions increase individual investment in deeply personal ways. While statistics can be convincing, they are far less memorable and effective at provoking action than emotions. Good stories can move people from a position of knowledge to a position of empathy—from appreciating a situation to actually caring about it (Patterson et al., 2008). "Stories," Patterson and his partners (2008) argue, "provide every person, no matter how limited his or her resources, with an influence tool that is both immediately accessible and enormously powerful" (Kindle location 1259).

In this chapter, we look at the characteristics of memorable stories. First, we explain how simplicity, unexpectedness, concreteness, credibility, and emotions can be used to create influential narratives. Then, we explore how new media tools—handheld cameras, video editing applications, and online image and video collections—are changing the ways that content creators attempt to influence audiences. Finally, we introduce a set of tips and tricks designed to help teachers effectively integrate visual persuasion into their classrooms.

Ideas That Are Made to Stick

Remember when your mother warned you that the chewing gum you swallowed would stay in your stomach for seven years? She was wrong. Your gum may not have been fully digested when it left your body, but it definitely left your body before seven years were up! What about the warning that your friend passed along about gang members killing drivers who flashed their lights after dark? That was a myth, too—so you can start using your high beams again. And the next six junk emails that land in your inbox warning of the catastrophic effects of nail polish, the plot to blow up the local shopping mall next Friday, or the dangers in consuming Pop Rocks are all urban legends too—but that won't stop your colleagues from forwarding them along and believing them with an almost foolhardy conviction, will it?

So what is it about these ideas that can cause otherwise intelligent people to suspend logic and believe? Research done by Chip Heath and Dan Heath (2007) at Stanford University suggests that the most influential individuals apply the following five principles—principles that appear again and again in urban legends—to actively create stories with stickiness and staying power.

1. **Simplicity:** Too many ideas get bogged down in the details. By trying to say everything, we end up saying nothing at all. Stickiness depends on our willingness to strip away our thinking until we find a small handful of core principles to share with audiences.

2. **Unexpectedness:** Audiences, particularly in the information-soaked world that we live in, rarely pay attention. Why listen to a speaker or follow a presentation when you are convinced that you can find the same information in half the time online? Capturing attention depends on appealing to curiosity—and curiosity is piqued by the unexpected.

3. **Concreteness:** Any teacher who has ever struggled to understand his or her school's mission statement understands that ambiguity kills ideas. While lofty ideals and language can sound really good on paper, messages that define tangible actions or appeal to the senses are more likely to have a long-term impact.

4. **Credibility:** Advertising agencies learned long ago that celebrity can add credibility to any message. The result: a never-ending parade of product endorsements and commercials. The average person crafting messages for audiences, though, must rely on a more practical version of credibility. Their ideas must be approachable and ready to test.

5. **Emotion:** Can you really blame your mother for making you throw away pounds of Halloween candy based on nothing more than the notion that neighbors were sliding razor blades into apples and poisoning Halloween candy? Fear for your safety—perhaps the strongest emotion that a mother can hold for her children—drove her actions. The best messengers recognize that when audiences feel, rather than simply think, they are more likely to remember.

The challenge for the modern storyteller, however, is that digital media has fundamentally changed the medium through which stories are told.

The Visual Content Explosion

Paralleling the rapid expansion of broadband Internet access, the availability of mobile devices, the rise of digital video recorders, the growth of the gaming industry, and the decreasing costs of personal video and photography equipment, access to—and engagement with—visual content exploded in the first decade of the 21st century.

YouTube (www.youtube.com)—the first online video warehouse to gain widespread popularity with Internet users—now sees one hundred hours of new content uploaded to its servers every minute. That shouldn't be surprising, given that one billion unique users visit the site every month, watching a total of six billion hours of video (YouTube, n.d.). Still, YouTube remains an underdog when it comes to the world of visual influence. "Our average user spends 15 minutes a day on the site," argues Hunter Walk, YouTube's director of product management. "They spend about five hours in front of the television. People say, 'YouTube is so big,' but I really see that we have a ways to go" (Helft, 2009).

More than 85 percent of all connected Americans watch online videos, totaling almost 31 billion views each month. That's an astounding monthly average of 182 online videos per user (Lipsman, 2010). Add the ever-expanding number of Internet users accessing video content on smartphones and tablet devices—mobile users make up almost 40 percent of YouTube's global watch time—and the impact of video content is only going to grow over time (YouTube, n.d.).

Understanding that video content resonates, marketers are investing in complex visual advertising programs that are capturing online attention. When bottled water company Evian wanted to put the brakes on its rapidly declining sales, they turned to a French advertising company, who promptly created a one-minute clip of roller-skating babies (http://snipurl.com/evianbabies) that was viewed 45 million times in its first six months, making it one of the most watched online commercials of all time (Sage, 2009). And when Zappos—a successful online shoe company catering to the young and trendy—wanted to make a digital splash and draw attention to its new line of clothing, they turned to a streaking nudist running through the streets of New York City wearing nothing more than sneakers and a "strategically positioned frontward fanny pack" (Newman, 2009). The videos—posted first on YouTube (http://snipurl.com/zapposad)—have been viewed tens of thousands of times, drawing the attention of major media outlets like CNN and the *Huffington Post* (Newman, 2009).

Blendtec—a company selling high-end blenders—has gotten into the visual influence game as well, designing a series of surprising videos starring an intentionally geeky presenter using the company's signature line of products to destroy items ranging from iPhones and two-by-fours to glow sticks and camcorders, videos that have increased sales by 20 percent (Li & Bernoff, 2008). Even ultraconservative companies like Lands' End and L.L.Bean are pushing away from an overreliance on traditional print marketing programs. In an attempt to be seen as more hip—and to attract younger consumers who rarely shop from catalogs—both companies are creating video shorts designed to advertise new lines of clothing that are being posted on store-dedicated YouTube channels. "It's a different step forward for us, but one that makes sense for where this customer shops," recognizes Lands' End president Nick Coe (Smith, 2009).

The Internet has even changed how people remember the most traditional content: news stories. The beginning-to-end broadcast models that newspapers, magazines, and radio and television programs have relied on for centuries are woefully ineffective at communicating information to the iGeneration. Instead, content that is remembered is interactive, providing users with opportunities to see streaming video or to independently explore related content (Tapscott, 2009). Responding to this reality, traditional media outlets invested early and often in video content—an action that paid off: almost 40 percent of adult Internet users watch news videos online (Madden, 2007).

Video wasn't the only type of visual content to explode in the first decade of the 21st century. Smartphones with high resolution cameras led to a revolution in digital photography. Flickr (www .flickr.com), one of the web's first photo sharing services, sees nearly 1 million photos uploaded every day—numbers that are dwarfed by the 60 million photos shared daily on Instagram (http:// instagram.com) and the 350 million new photos uploaded to Facebook every day (Etherington, 2014; Instagram, n.d.; Smith, 2013). Combined with the content created by users of similar services like Pinterest (www.pinterest.com) and Tumblr (www.tumblr.com), digital photographers are uploading almost six thousand digital images to the web per minute (Meeker, 2013). And individuals aren't the only ones using photo services to reach new audiences. By the fall of 2014, 72 percent of prestige brands—think Nike, Starbucks, and BMW—were creating and sharing visual content on Instagram, drawing the attention of millions of followers (Gillett, 2014; TOTEMS, n.d.).

The lesson to be learned: influence in the new media ecology is dependent on more than creating sticky stories. Influence in the new media ecology is dependent on the ability to create sticky stories communicated through powerful digital images and videos.

Initial Attempts at Visual Influence

Thankfully, the same kinds of characteristics that define traditionally influential stories—simplicity, concreteness, unexpectedness, credibility, and emotion—also define the most memorable images and videos. Evian, Zappos, and Blendtec—the three companies recognized earlier for their innovative video advertisements—created short, simple bits that played on the unexpected. Roller-skating babies, confident nudists, and exceptionally destructive blenders are not everyday occurrences for most people, after all. Each video was set in a familiar location, however, and features intentionally ordinary characters that viewers can relate to, lending an element of concreteness to the advertisements. Finally, it is almost impossible to watch any of these videos without laughing out loud, and humor is almost always memorable to viewers (Cashmore, 2009).

Contrary to popular belief, structuring visual influence projects in your classroom *shouldn't* begin with a video camera. Instead, structuring visual influence projects should begin by crafting messages built around still images. While video can be more captivating, it requires a set of technical skills that most teachers and students new to digital projects will struggle with. Using familiar applications like PowerPoint or Canva (www.canva.com) to design a single influential slide is a far more approachable task because most teachers and students are comfortable with the basic steps involved in creating stand-alone images. Similarly, using applications like Easel.ly (www.easel.ly) to develop infographics—images that represent data, statistics, and ideas in a graphic form—can serve as a motivating starting point for visual influence projects. Students designing infographics learn to tell stories about concepts that are easy to read and that lead to more inquiry.

Whether you have students creating stand-alone images with PowerPoint, Canva, or Easel.ly, the ability to produce motivating final products quickly builds momentum for any attempt to introduce students to the skills of visual influence. But don't be fooled. While most of the students in your classroom are likely to be comfortable with—even bored by—the basic features of these tools, few will have had any formal instruction in the careful composition of influential visuals. Instead, after years of creating presentations with little guidance, most students create slides that are hard to follow, poorly organized, and filled with distractions. They will choose background colors and font styles that are difficult to read and inappropriate for the intended audience. They will overuse transitions between slides and bullet points, convinced that anything moving is engaging. They will include too much text, too many clip art images, and too many sounds.

Breaking these habits begins by sharing several samples of influential images with your classes. They must learn to strip away the frills typically found in student-created graphics and focus instead on the simple, unexpected, concrete, credible, and emotional content that Chip and Dan Heath argue is the most influential. Memorable visual images do the following.

- **Use powerful images as backgrounds:** Digital photography has become increasingly popular and accessible in the past decade and people willingly share their images with the world. With a bit of searching, students can find beautiful pictures to use as the centerpiece of their visual images. Stressing the important role that the right picture or graphic can play in changing people's minds can almost instantly improve the quality of the messages that your students are creating.

- **Include memorable catchphrases:** Can you complete the following sentences? "Help Woodsy spread the word. Never be a _____." "Oscar Meyer has a way with _____." "Have a Coke and a _____." Birds, bologna, and smiles have never been the same, have they? They are paired forever with short, memorable catchphrases that were used in clever marketing campaigns. The most influential messages follow the same course of action, relying on a handful of carefully crafted words instead of overwhelming amounts of text-based evidence.

- **Are visually appealing:** Few students make careful decisions about colors, icons, and text shapes, sizes, and layouts when creating their own visuals. Instead, they are drawn to shocking colors and Word Art. Teachers must show students how colors, contrasts, and placement decisions can be used to make individual words and messages stand out without turning visual images into sloppy creations that turn viewers off.

At the end of this chapter, you can find an activity titled "The Characteristics of Memorable Images" (page 83) that can be used to introduce your students to the characteristics of the best visual images. It asks students to answer a series of questions based on the work of Chip and Dan Heath about two different images designed to influence thinking on global poverty. After working through this activity, students should have a better sense of the elements of persuasive visuals and be ready to create their own influential digital images. The handout "Checklist for Creating Influential Visual Images" (page 85) can structure their efforts. Finally, students can use the "Influential Visual Image Scoring Rubric" (page 87) to provide one another with feedback on the quality of their finished products.

A Word About Creative Commons

One of the best lessons that can be taught in projects on visual influence and persuasion is that images, music tracks, and videos all carry the same kinds of copyright protections as text. While students generally understand that lifting content from a book, article, or encyclopedia without citing the original source is bad practice, they are far less careful when creating multimedia products. The results are presentations filled with content quickly drawn from Google searches. Visual influence assignments, then, are natural opportunities to introduce your students to the concept of digital authorship and attribution.

The first step in preparing your students to use multimedia content responsibly is to introduce them to Creative Commons. Drawn from the open-source movement, in which software developers make their code openly available and allow others to freely change what was once considered proprietary content, Creative Commons is a nonprofit corporation founded in 2001 with the intent of making it easier for digital authors to share their final products. In the first eight years of its existence, over 130 million works were licensed under Creative Commons (n.d.b).

When a digital author creates a piece of content and decides to freely share it with others, he or she has six different Creative Commons licenses to choose from. Like traditional citations, every Creative Commons license requires attribution; anyone using Creative Commons content must give credit to the original creator of the piece he or she has chosen to use. In addition, digital authors can set the following conditions on the use of their content (Creative Commons, n.d.a).

- **Attribution Share Alike:** This license gives users permission to use or change a digital author's original content however they like—including for commercial purposes. By using this license, digital authors guarantee that their original content will always remain open for use by others. They also promote Creative Commons by requiring that new versions of their original works remain free and open to others as well.

- **Attribution No Derivatives:** This license gives users permission to share or publish a piece of content created by a digital author as long as the original work remains unchanged and proper credit is given.

- **Attribution Non-Commercial:** This license gives users permission to use or change a digital author's original content however they like as long as any new pieces created are being used for noncommercial purposes. Using the Attribution Non-Commercial license ensures digital authors that others are not making money off of their original works.

- **Attribution Non-Commercial Share Alike:** Similar to the Attribution Non-Commercial license, this license gives users permission to use or change a digital author's original content however they like as long as the new pieces are being used for noncommercial purposes and remain free for others to use in the same way. Not only do digital authors who select the Attribution Non-Commercial Share Alike license ensure that no one makes money off of their original works, they actively promote continued contributions to Creative Commons.

Creative Commons content is easy to find on the Internet. Pieces licensed under Creative Commons will usually be clearly identified with statements or icons found in headers, footers, and sidebars. Using the advanced options of popular search engines like Google, users can sort images, videos, and music results by license. Users can also use the free search tool on the Creative Commons website (http://search.creativecommons.org) to tap into the most popular sources of content licensed under the Creative Commons. Finally, there are several online Creative Commons warehouses that users can turn to when looking for content for multimedia projects. Some of the best include the following.

- **Foter** (http://foter.com): Foter is fast becoming one of the most popular sources for students interested in finding Creative Commons images. Housing a collection of over three hundred million images sorted into categories to make searching easier (buildings, babies, holidays, signs, sports, technology), Foter makes determining the type of license attached to each image and giving credit to the original content creator easy.

- **Flickr Creative Commons** (www.flickr.com/creativecommons): While teachers and district technology leaders are often concerned about the ability of users to find inappropriate content on Flickr, it is a site with an absolutely incredible collection of images that photographers have made available under Creative Commons licenses. With proper coaching and supervision, students can use Flickr to easily find engaging visual content for any project.

- **Wikimedia** (http://commons.wikimedia.org): Despite the criticism that they take from educators concerned about reliability of online sources, Wikipedia users are some of the most open content creators in the world. The Wikimedia website contains a collection of images and videos posted in Wikipedia that are often copyright free.

- **morgueFile** (www.morguefile.com): Like Wikimedia, morgueFile is designed as a warehouse of copyright-free images. The photographers who share their images in morgueFile are working to create a set of reference images on common topics for the world to use. They take great satisfaction in lowering the barrier to incorporating high-quality photography into school-related projects and often only request an image citation or an email for a picture to be used.

- **Jamendo** (www.jamendo.com): Music plays a prominent role in the lives of our students, which makes the selection of background tracks one of the most exciting parts of any visual influence project. Providing access to the work of independent artists in nearly every genre, Jamendo is one of the best sources for music licensed under Creative Commons.

- **ccMixter** (http://ccmixter.org): ccMixter is another great source of background music for students working on visual influence projects. What makes ccMixter interesting, however, is that it actively encourages users to remix tracks created by others, giving students an inside look into what Creative Commons content is all about. ccMixter provides access to a range of different sound effects and ambient noises that can be used in digital projects as well.

Introducing your students to content licensed by Creative Commons is an important first step toward encouraging digital responsibility. By making use of Creative Commons content, your students will begin to see those who produce non-text-based content as authors with ideas worth protecting too—an important lesson for anyone interested in visual influence.

Digital Storytelling

Once students have honed their skills creating influential still images, they are ready to begin experimenting with digital storytelling. Digital stories use images, music, narrative, and voice to bring characters, situations, and ideas to life. The best digital stories are often structured similarly to traditional stories—with a sense of tension and conflict developed through a clear beginning, middle, and ending. Like any influential idea, the best digital stories play on senses and emotions to make abstract concepts, experiences, and beliefs tangible and concrete.

For students, learning to create influential multimedia expressions is exciting because it resembles the kinds of storytelling that they are surrounded by every day—and this excitement pays dividends for classroom teachers willing to experiment with video. Digital storytelling requires students to interact with content at a much deeper level than more conventional forms of storytelling. Communicating through text is a relatively straightforward process for traditional authors, who use only words to engage with audiences. Digital storytellers, however, need to consider how images and music—combined with lighting, camera angles, transitions, and colors—can be used to emphasize key points and move audiences to act. Learning to use these tools together to craft a unified message requires a nuanced understanding of a concept.

Your first digital storytelling projects should begin in the same digital photography warehouses that your students used when creating influential still images. By eliminating video footage from your earliest digital storytelling projects, you simplify an editing process that can be overwhelming for both you and your students and focus attention on the content necessary to create influential messages (Davidson, 2004). While your students may be convinced that they are ready to script and stage their own scenes, complete with voice-over narration and sound effects from day one, they stand a better chance at gaining influence if their early attempts require nothing more than selecting and arranging a series of digital images into a convincing narrative and then adding a background track to generate interest and emotion.

Multimedia expert Hall Davidson (2004) argues this scaffolding process should start with teachers putting together digital kits for their classes that contain all of the pieces necessary for creating influential videos:

> What replaces the camcorder in the classroom is a folder of curriculum-based images, sounds, and narratives. They sit together in a kit like a jigsaw puzzle, ready to be assembled by students. . . . Building videos means assembling video, audio, and story elements—including writing. With digital video, all of these elements can be prefabricated for final student assembly. The notion of scaffolding is the idea the teacher supplies elements for use during the early stages of a project.

Creating digital kits for your classes—which are typically organized by topic and posted online, uploaded to shared folders on district networks—can also speed up the process of video creation, a primary concern of teachers working with new tools or in schools with limited access to digital resources. Students can practice creating influential visual messages without investing hundreds of hours independently digging through source material. Better yet, complete digital kits mean that students need less direct supervision from their teachers to create videos—an important consideration in classes with twenty-five to thirty students. As Davidson (2004) writes:

> When the construction kit is simple and complete, assembling an impressive looking digital video is much easier than in the days of in-camera editing. The margin for error is also smaller when all the necessary parts are already there. No matter how simple the assembly, students will learning [sic] the basic editing skills they will need as they move to more sophisticated and original projects.

To preserve student choice, however, and to better measure levels of student mastery in your room, consider filling each digital kit with a wide range of content to choose from. Along with high-quality items, select images and music that are deeply powerful but communicate the wrong emotions. Find content that is incredibly tactile as well as content that fails to appeal to any senses. Include detailed voice-over narration clips or text-based graphics that might look convincing but fail to focus on a few key points. Doing so will result in a range of interesting final projects and can help you better assess what your students know and can do.

Once you have designed a digital kit that can be used to create a powerful story on the topic you are studying in class, it is time to introduce students to a few key organizing points that they should consider when assembling their videos. These organizing points—which are detailed in the "Planning Template for Influential Videos" found on page 89—include the following actions.

- **Cluster slides:** Even when students rely heavily on images for the body of their videos, a central organizing strategy is necessary. Students should be sure to cluster related facts, images, and graphics by category when assembling their final products. Viewers will then see the logical progression of the content.

- **Use catchphrases as transitions:** Remember that simple phrases highlighting key points can serve as cornerstones for influential ideas. Students can be taught to craft and then use these simple phrases throughout their videos as transitions that emphasize main ideas repeatedly throughout a presentation. The best place to use catchphrases is at the end of each cluster of slides. That way, viewers will know when images or facts on a new subcategory are about to appear.

- **Establish a content rhythm:** Presenting content in a clear pattern makes communicating a main idea much easier. When viewers can predict what is going to come next, they spend more time focused on ideas and less time focused on presentation details. Some content rhythm patterns that may work for student presentations built from digital kits include: Fact, Fact, Catchphrase, Image; Image, Fact, Fact, Image, Catchphrase; or Image, Image, Fact, Image, Image, Fact.

Convincing students that clustering, catchphrases, and content rhythms matter can often be a challenge in and of itself. While the best videos all include some form of organization and structure, these elements are rarely transparent and obvious to viewers. To tackle this challenge, consider using the "Examining a Video" activity found on page 90, which asks students to reflect on a video focused on global poverty titled *Poverty's Real* (http://bit.ly/smskivavideo) created by middle schoolers using a digital kit.

After students are comfortable with the content they have collected, it is time to introduce an editing application that can be used to publish videos. While there are several different applications—both software and web based—that can be used to arrange and publish videos, most share the following features in common.

- **The ability to import content from external sources:** The first step that students will have to take when assembling their final videos is to point their editing application to any content—images, graphics, audio files—they are planning to use in their final product. Most applications enable users to create folders for each new project.

- **The ability to "storyboard" video content:** Storyboards are graphic organizers used to sequence content in developing video projects. In editing applications, these graphic organizers generally allow users to click and drag any visual content—still images, videos, graphics—into place. They also tend to allow users to easily insert transitions between clips in a developing presentation.

- **The ability to publish final copies in multiple formats:** Once users have selected and organized the images, audio files, and transitions they would like to include in their videos, most editing applications will publish final copies in any number of formats. Guided by a series of simple questions that help determine the right format for the intended purpose of the project, students can ask editing applications to render videos appropriate for playing online, on full-sized computers, or on handheld devices like smartphones or tablets. Most video editing applications also make it possible for users to post final products directly to popular web-based video warehouses like YouTube.

- **Ensure online and offline capability:** New low-cost computers like Google's Chromebook require online access for most resources to be used, but some applications also allow the students to work offline. Some students might not have online access at home, so offline capabilities for editing will be required. Resources such as WeVideo (www.wevideo.com) and the offline version of the Chrome app WeVideo Next are great examples of an online and offline editing tool.

One of the best editing applications for students creating videos from digital kits is Animoto (https://animoto.com/education/classroom). After uploading and organizing collections of still images and short video clips, Animoto users can choose a background track from a large collection of songs licensed for use under Creative Commons. Then, users can make several simple editing choices—selecting a theme, spotlighting individual images, deciding how fast images will transition in a video. When users are happy with their choices, Animoto adds impressive transitions between each image and publishes a final product directly to the web. By automating much of the video production process and by providing users with ready access to a library of songs that can be used freely in videos, Animoto makes it possible for users with little technical skill to quickly create highly polished final products.

A scoring rubric and a teacher planning checklist for video-based influence projects is included at the end of this chapter (pages 92–96).

Final Thoughts

When he started teaching language arts to middle grade students ten years ago, George Mayo of Silver Springs, Maryland, had no real intentions of becoming a leading expert in using video in teaching and learning. He just knew that a part of his curriculum required students to learn about the elements of good stories—conflicts, characters, mood, tone—and that another part of his curriculum required students to learn about to the elements of persuasion. Most importantly, though, George knew that the key to teaching his students these very traditional skills rested in a nontraditional medium for communication. "Students love video," he argues. "Student motivation and interest goes up when you give them the chance to create video-based projects. They also love to use technology. When set up correctly, video-based projects promote higher order thinking skills" (G. Mayo, personal communication, January 2, 2010).

For George, setting up multimedia projects correctly begins with providing real structure for students, who are often tackling new tasks for the first time. The best projects depend on objectives and guidelines that clearly define the ideas and concepts to be included in final products. Students also need to know exactly what kind of finished piece they must create—an influential still image, a video built from a digital kit, a public service announcement—and have access to samples that can be used as models. "Make sure you give students plenty of time at the beginning of the project to brainstorm," George writes. "If students invest time and effort coming up with a solid plan, they are more vested in the final product. The groups that do not adequately plan at the start tend to have to hardest time getting to the finish line" (G. Mayo, personal communication, January 2, 2010).

Finally, successful multimedia projects may just depend on teachers' willingness to find additional time to support their students. It is not always possible for classes to master new skills inside the typical fifty-minute period—especially when those skills require sophisticated interactions with content and tools. Offering to work with students before school, during school-wide enrichment periods, and after school can ensure that groups experience success. Sometimes, the best strategy is to start with a small handful of motivated students—a group needing differentiation, an after-school club, or a digital lunch bunch—who can help work the kinks out of new digital projects before they are widely introduced across classes, teams, or grade levels (G. Mayo, personal communication, January 2, 2010).

While structuring successful multimedia projects may seem like an intimidating proposition at first, for George, the benefits are well worth it:

> Challenging projects help to build a strong classroom community. . . . Students inevitably end up supporting each other as the project progresses and tech "experts" start to stand out and offer their help to groups who need it. We always share our work as a class when we're finished, and the students love seeing what others have created. There's a real sense of accomplishment when we complete our digital stories, and that's fun to see! (G. Mayo, personal communication, January 2, 2010)

In the end, we simply can't ignore images and video as a medium for communication any longer. While our schools may remain text-driven institutions, our students are surrounded by visual messages the moment they walk out of our classrooms. Learning to be creators rather than simply consumers of this engaging content is an essential first step towards being influential in tomorrow's world.

Curriculum Matters: The ISTE Standards for Students

The standards defined by the International Society for Technology in Education (ISTE) expect students to "create original works as a means of personal and group expression" (ISTE, n.d.). This means that students should be able to communicate effectively in a variety of media and formats, to use digital content and tools ethically and responsibly, and to select the right digital tools to complete individual tasks (ISTE, n.d.).

Do these skills also appear in the curricula for your classes? Are they skills that you believe are important for iGeners? Which activities, strategies, and tools presented in this chapter would help students master these skills?

The Characteristics of Memorable Images

One of the first steps toward creating powerful visual messages is to examine images created by others. In this activity, students are asked to use the criteria outlined in *Made to Stick* (Heath & Heath, 2007) to evaluate two separate images designed to provoke thinking around the issue of global poverty.

Image 1

Source: Adapted from "Homeless in Sugamo 1" by james-fischer. Creative Commons, 2006.

Image 2

Source: Adapted from "Save Our Children" by rachdian. Creative Commons, 2009.

Questions for Consideration

1. Like any content, both of these images have strengths and weaknesses. Begin by listing everything that you like about image 1. What is most impressive to you? Least impressive? If you were to change anything about image 1, what would it be?

    Then, answer the same questions about image 2.

2. The most influential messages are simple. They are stripped down, sharing only core principles and key ideas. Which of these images does a better job at sharing a small handful of core principles with viewers? What would you do to make the more complicated image simpler?

3. The most influential messages are unexpected, either communicating with audiences in a nontraditional way or sharing ideas that are startling. Is there anything surprising about either of these images? What impact does that have on you as a viewer?

4. The most influential messages are concrete. Instead of sharing complicated language, they appeal to the basic senses of the audience. Which of these two images does a better job appealing to your senses?

5. The most influential messages are credible. The ideas shared must be believable to viewers. Something about the message has to resonate with an audience's experiences. Which of these two images can you relate to better? Why?

6. The most influential messages are emotional, making viewers feel instead of simply think. Influential people know that when they can tap into powerful emotions, their ideas are more likely to be remembered. Which of these images does a better job of making you feel instead of just think? What emotions does it evoke?

7. When crafting visual messages, the layout, size, and color of all fonts and images are incredibly important. The best visual images appear balanced and clean to viewers, rather than distracting. How do you think the authors of these two slides did at creating balanced, clean images?

Source: Heath, C., & Heath, D. (2007). Made to stick: Why some ideas survive and others die. *New York: Random House.*

Checklist for Creating Influential Visual Images

Creating influential visual images requires careful attention to the key elements of memorable ideas. Use this checklist to help think through the visual image you are required to create on the topic we are studying in class.

Questions to Consider

1. Describe your intended audience for this visual. What are they likely to know already about the topic we are studying? How are they likely to feel about the topic?

2. How do you want your audience to feel about the topic? What do you want them to know or do after they finish seeing your visual?

3. What information can you share about the topic that is likely to be the most convincing to your audience? What information is likely to be the most surprising? Are there any bits of evidence that you think your audience will find convincing *and* surprising?

4. If you had to summarize your own feelings about the topic in one sentence or less, what would your summary look like? Can you craft this one sentence summary into a memorable catchphrase for your visual?

5. Have you visited a Creative Commons warehouse (listed at the bottom of this checklist) and selected several potential images to use in your visual? Have you copied and pasted the source for your image into a works cited page?

6. Which image carries the strongest emotions? How does the image make you feel? Have you checked with several of your peers to see if the image makes them feel the same way? Are the emotions shared in your image the emotions that you are trying to share about the topic?

7. What senses—touch, taste, sight, sound, smell—are conveyed the best in your image? How are those senses communicated? Will viewers be able to feel what the characters in the picture are feeling? Why?

8. Have you chosen an image or graphic that will carry some familiarity for your viewers? What about the circumstances portrayed will they be able to relate to?

9. Where are you going to place the text in your visual? Do you have enough room for all of your text to be seen easily from a distance? Are you planning on using colors and text sizes to draw attention to individual words or ideas? Which ones? Have you selected a font that won't be distracting?

Warehouses for Creative Commons Images

Photographers who share their work in the following image warehouses allow others to use their content in digital projects as long as they are given credit. Use these warehouses to look for content to use in your influential visual.

Wikimedia

Wikimedia (http://commons.wikimedia.org) connects to a collection of images and videos posted in Wikipedia that are often copyright free—or are free for use in most situations with nothing more than a citation of the original source.

morgueFile

morgueFile (www.morguefile.com) is designed as a warehouse of images that are copyright free and available to any user for any project with little restriction. The photographers who share their images in morgueFile are working to create a set of reference images on common topics for the world to use.

Flickr Creative Commons

Images found in Flickr's Creative Commons gallery (www.flickr.com/creativecommons) can be used for almost any project related to education with nothing more than a credit to the original photographer.

Foter

Housing a collection of over three hundred million images sorted into categories to make searching easier (buildings, babies, holidays, signs, sports, technology), Foter (www.foter.com) makes determining the type of license attached to each image and giving credit to the original content creator easy.

Influential Visual Image Scoring Rubric

When rating an influential visual, three categories are important to consider: the content included, the production enhancements that make the visual more engaging, and the overall appearance of the final product. The following rubric will help you determine the quality of your influential visual. *Content* refers to the statistics, facts, statements, and quotations used to introduce the issue to viewers. *Production* and *enhancements* refer to the fonts, colors, and images used to evoke emotions and to polish a presentation. *Overall appearance* refers to the general sense communicated by the final product as a whole.

Basic	Intermediate	Advanced
Content		
Content is often inaccurate. Facts must be checked again. The language used to deliver content is inappropriate for this audience. Audiences will struggle to make sense of the issue being presented because of inaccurate or insufficient content. Audiences are unlikely to be interested in this issue after viewing this final product.	Content is accurate but not especially engaging. Better fact selection would have improved the value of the final product. Content is delivered in language that is appropriate for the intended audience. Audiences are left with unanswered questions about why this issue matters. Audiences may enjoy this presentation but are unlikely to be moved to action.	Content included is accurate and engaging. Content paints a moving picture of the issue being presented. Content is delivered in language that is appropriate for the intended audience. Audiences are drawn into this issue and moved to action by the content.
Production/Enhancements		
The image chosen may seem unrelated to the issue being studied. Source for the image chosen has not been included. Little has been done to use fonts, colors, text sizes, or images to enhance the final product. Final product comes across as careless and amateurish to audience.	The fonts, colors, and text sizes chosen make learning from the final product possible. Source for the image has been included but may not be free from copyright protections. The fonts, colors, text sizes, and image selected for this final product are interesting but may not always communicate the appropriate emotions. The final product is a strong student sample, but few would describe it as professional.	Fonts, colors, and text sizes have been used to emphasize critical ideas in this final product. Source for the image has been included, is publicly available, and is licensed for use under Creative Commons. Image has been carefully selected to evoke an emotional response from viewers. Final product has a professional look and feel that engages viewers. Viewers will easily remember this final product.

page 1 of 2

Basic	Intermediate	Advanced
Overall Appearance		
Final product includes too much text, text that is poorly sized, or fonts that are unreadable when shared with an audience. Quality of the image is poor. Image is poorly sized, distorted, too dark, or too light. There appears to be no logical layout to the final product. Content and images appear to be scattered, making the message hard to follow. The use of word art and clip art is unprofessional, distracting viewers from the intended message of the final product.	Final product includes an appropriate amount of text that is clearly visible and easy to read when shared with an audience. The quality of the image shared is average. While the image is generally undistorted, it may distract viewers or be inappropriate for the intended message of the final product. There is a clear organization to the final product, but the organization may be ineffective, causing the viewer to work in order to understand the intended message of the final product. If word art or clip art have been used, it has been done appropriately and does not distract viewers.	Text has been carefully chosen, communicating important ideas in as few words as possible. As a result, the final product is clearly visible, easy to read when shared with an audience, and very informative. The image shared is extraordinary. Not only is it undistorted and appropriate for the intended message of the final product, but it is also powerful and engaging. The organizational strategy for the final product is effective. Important content stands out without confusion. Word art and clip art have not been used. Instead, the intended message is communicated through powerful words, clean fonts, and an interesting image.

Planning Template for Influential Videos

The best videos require careful planning and structure. Use this template to begin thinking through the final product you are trying to create.

What is the **topic** of your video? Can you think of a clever title for your video?

What **emotions** are you trying to convey in your video? How do you want your readers to feel when they are finished watching your video?

Slide clusters are groups of images, statistics, quotes, and facts about one related concept. They act like paragraphs in a video, helping organize ideas and guide viewers through a story. What concepts could you create slide clusters around in your video?

Catchphrases are simple phrases that emphasize main ideas repeatedly throughout a presentation or serve as a transition from one cluster of slides to the next. What catchphrases would work well for your video?

Content rhythms are clear patterns in the way that images, facts, quotes, and statistics appear in a video. They make it easy for a viewer to follow a video and predict what is coming next. A content rhythm might look like this: Fact, Fact, Catchphrase, Image. What content rhythm would work well for your video?

Examining a Video

One of the first steps you should take before creating your own influential video is to carefully examine a digital story created by other students. Spend a few minutes answering the following questions while watching *Poverty's Real* (http://bit.ly/smskivavideo), a video created by middle schoolers that is designed to introduce viewers to global poverty.

Questions to Consider

1. Begin by watching the *Poverty's Real* video from beginning to end. What emotion does the video attempt to convey? How are the authors trying to make you feel about global poverty?

2. Now, watch *Poverty's Real* a second time. What kind of content have the authors used to try to influence their audience? How has that content been organized?

3. Are there any logical categories or segments in the video? Are there any patterns in the way content is presented that viewers can pick up on?

4. In a written piece, authors use transitions between paragraphs to signal to readers that ideas and arguments are changing. How do the digital authors of *Poverty's Real* indicate that ideas are changing? What impact does this decision have on viewers?

5. Videos require digital authors to use more than just images to communicate messages. Text sizes, colors, and digital effects like transitions can also help set the mood and lend structure to a piece. How have the digital authors of *Poverty's Real* used these kinds of visual elements?

6. It would be hard to watch *Poverty's Real* without being drawn to the music, but does it support the general message of the video? Are the words and beat appropriate? Why?

7. What lessons can you learn about effective digital messages from *Poverty's Real*? Are there any strategies that you will try to replicate in your own work?

8. What will you remember the most about *Poverty's Real*? Do you think that was the message the digital authors wanted you to remember the most?

Teaching the iGeneration © 2010, 2015 Solution Tree Press • solution-tree.com
Visit **go.solution-tree.com/technology** or **plugusin.pbworks.com** to download this page.

Influential Video Scoring Rubric

When rating an influential video, three categories are important to consider: the content that has been included, the delivery and sequencing of the presentation, and the digital enhancements that make the visual production more engaging. The following rubric will help you determine the quality of your final product. *Content* refers to the statistics, facts, and quotations used to introduce the issue to viewers. *Delivery* and *sequencing* refer to the structure used to introduce content to viewers. *Production* and *enhancements* refer to the fonts, colors, images, transitions, and background music used to evoke emotions and to polish a presentation.

Basic	Intermediate	Advanced
Content		
Content is often inaccurate. Facts must be checked again. The language used to deliver content is inappropriate for this audience. Sources for content are not shared, are out of date, or are unreliable. Audiences will struggle to make sense of the issue being presented because of inaccurate or insufficient content. Audiences are unlikely to be interested in this issue after viewing the presentation.	Content is accurate but limited. More detail would have improved the value of the final product. Content is delivered in language that is appropriate for the intended audience. Some of the sources for content are not entirely clear or reliable. Audiences are left with unanswered questions about why this issue matters. Audiences may enjoy this presentation but are unlikely to be moved to action.	Content included is accurate and engaging. Content paints a thorough and complete picture of the issue being introduced. Sources for content are reliable, current, and shared with audience. Content is delivered in language that is appropriate for the intended audience. Audiences are drawn into this issue and moved to action by content.

Basic	Intermediate	Advanced
Delivery/Sequencing		
There does not appear to be a logical pattern for sequencing content, leaving viewers confused. While all content presented is connected to the same issue, statistics, facts, statements, and quotations appear to haphazardly wander across a range of subtopics and categories. Presentation may seem incredibly short or painfully long to the audience. Audiences will struggle to learn from this presentation and will find viewing a chore.	A logical plan for delivery and an effective sequencing of content is clear to viewers. Most content has been broken into obvious subtopics and categories that are evident to audiences. A few statistics, facts, statements, or quotations seem misplaced, potentially confusing audiences. Presentation is an appropriate length and will hold the attention of the audience. Audiences could learn from this presentation without challenge.	Delivery and sequencing of content is carefully focused and structured, making it highly likely that viewers can learn new content easily from this presentation. Content has been broken into obvious subtopics and categories that are clearly evident to audiences. Audience is so engaged by the content, delivery, and sequencing that they are disappointed when the presentation ends.
Production/Enhancements		
Little has been done to use fonts, colors, text sizes, background music, or images to enhance this presentation. Transitions may be overused or inappropriate for a professional finished product. Instead of moving viewers through a presentation, they become distractions. Presentation comes across as careless and amateurish to viewers.	The fonts, colors, and text sizes used make learning from the presentation possible. The background music and images selected for this presentation are interesting but may not always communicate the appropriate emotions. Transitions move viewers through the presentation without distraction. The presentation is a strong student product, but few would describe it as professional.	Fonts, colors, and text sizes have been used to emphasize critical ideas in this presentation. Background music lends a sense of clear and appropriate emotion to the issue being studied. Images have been carefully selected and organized to evoke emotional responses. Transitions are carefully selected and engaging, visually moving the audience through the presentation without causing distractions. Presentation has a professional look and feel.

Teacher Digital Video Checklist

While teacher- and student-created video projects are rapidly becoming a part of classrooms, they require careful planning and structure. This checklist can help you think through the kinds of technical and pedagogical questions that you will need to answer before video projects are successful in your classroom.

Technical and Procedural Preparations

1. Have you checked with your school or district's technology services specialists to ensure that your classroom or school computers can handle the demands of video editing and publishing?

    Your Response / Next Steps:

2. Have you checked with your school or district's technology services specialists to see which video editing applications are already installed on your classroom computers?

    Your Response / Next Steps:

3. If you are planning on using an online video editing application, have you made sure that the program you have chosen is on your district's approved software list?

    Your Response / Next Steps:

4. If you are planning on using an online video editing application, have you thought through how students will sign in to the program? Will they need individual user accounts? Will you create one account for your classes to share?

    Your Response / Next Steps:

5. Have you experimented with the key features of the video editing application that you are planning to use? Can you import content, storyboard videos, and add transitions, background tracks, and narration? Can you publish a final copy?

    Your Response / Next Steps:

6. Will your students be able to accomplish each of these video editing tasks without troubles? If not, are you planning on training a small handful of students to serve as technology helpers during your classroom video project?

   Your Response / Next Steps:

7. If you are planning on allowing students to use source material—images or video—that they generate, are you aware of your district's photo and video release policies? Have you thought through the ways that these policies will change the content that your students can collect?

   Your Response / Next Steps:

Pedagogical Preparations

1. Are you comfortable with the characteristics of influential ideas? Have you introduced these characteristics to your students?

   Your Response / Next Steps:

2. Are you planning on introducing several sample videos for your students to explore that demonstrate the characteristics of influential ideas in action? Where will you find these videos?

   Your Response / Next Steps:

3. Have you thought through the natural connections between your video project and other required outcomes in your curriculum? Are you going to be able to integrate this assignment into the work you are already doing? How?

   Your Response / Next Steps:

4. Are your students aware of and comfortable with using catchphrases, content rhythms, and slide clusters to add structure to their videos?

   Your Response / Next Steps:

Teaching the iGeneration © 2010, 2015 Solution Tree Press • solution-tree.com
Visit **go.solution-tree.com/technology** or **plugusin.pbworks.com** to download this page.

5. Are you planning on creating a digital kit for your students that includes images, graphics, music tracks, and voice-over narration connected to your topic? Will these digital kits include a wide range of content, allowing for student choice and providing you with better opportunities to assess student mastery of visual influence?

Your Response / Next Steps:

6. Will your digital kit include graphics—charts, graphs, statistics—connected to your topic? If so, have you collected these graphics?

Your Response / Next Steps:

7. If you are planning on allowing students to assemble their own digital kits, have you introduced Creative Commons and the responsible use of digital content? Have you identified potential sources where students can easily find images and video licensed under Creative Commons?

Your Response / Next Steps:

8. Have you thought through where your digital kits will be stored? If you are going to post all content online or in a folder on your school's shared network, have you taught students how to access those source folders? Can students access your digital kits from home if necessary?

Your Response / Next Steps:

CHAPTER **FOUR**

Exploring Collaborative Dialogue

Working at CERN—a physics laboratory employing thousands of people from around the world—in the late 1980s and early 1990s, Tim Berners-Lee had an all-too-common 21st century desire: to be able to effectively interact with coworkers regardless of their location, the types of computers they were using, or the format of files they were creating. Efficient interaction, Berners-Lee figured, would make everyone smarter because they would have access to shared information. Efficient interactions were impossible at that point in time, however, because there was no single standard for communication between computers and no easy way to meet with everyone individually. Determined to build a system that would enable connections to both information and individuals regardless of the devices that they were using, Berners-Lee created the World Wide Web (Gillies & Cailliau, 2000).

At first, Berners-Lee didn't have global intentions for his invention. His initial goal was simply to create a solution for the communication challenge he was facing in the workplace. "There was never a feeling of 'Heh, heh, heh, we can change the world,'" he said in a 2005 interview with the *Telegraph*. He said, "It was, 'This is exciting, it would be nice if this happened,' combined with a constant fear that it would not work out" ("Three Loud Cheers," 2005). It didn't take long for Berners-Lee to become convinced, however, that the World Wide Web had potential that could change the world in far more meaningful ways. He noted, "I'd like to see it building links between families in different countries . . . to allow us to browse people's websites in different languages so you can see how they live in different countries" ("Three Loud Cheers," 2005).

While Berners-Lee hasn't yet seen the World Wide Web being used to completely break down global barriers between countries, teens—who have always been driven to communicate—have wholeheartedly embraced the new opportunities to connect that are facilitated by the web. In fact, as of 2013, eight out of every ten Americans between the ages of twelve and seventeen had created accounts on social networking services like Twitter, Instagram, and Facebook (Madden et al.,

2013)—and most check their digital profiles *at least* once each day, connecting both with friends they see frequently and those they only see once in a while (Lenhart & Madden, 2007).

In social spaces, teens are managing existing relationships by making plans, sharing thoughts, touching base, sending public and private messages, commenting on one another's blogs, and posting on each other's profiles (Lenhart & Madden, 2007). They form groups around causes, and they give and take surveys. They build diverse core networks that they rely on for guidance and advice (Hampton, Sessions, Her, & Rainie, 2009). "By providing tools for mediated interactions," writes danah boyd (2010), "social media allow teens to extend their interactions beyond physical boundaries. Conversations and interactions that begin in person do not end when friends are separated" (p. 80).

Heavy skepticism surrounds social networking websites, however. Rather than seeing social spaces as highly motivating destinations for communication—a fundamental building block for learning—most parents and teachers see them as nothing more than forums for hurtful behaviors like gossiping and cyberbullying. We worry about time spent staring at digital profiles, convinced that our students are losing the social skills necessary for interacting in face-to-face environments. Worse yet, programs like NBC's *To Catch a Predator* and PBS's *Growing Up Online* have left us questioning how safe our students really are on the Internet.

The consequence of this skepticism, argues social learning consultant Steve Hargadon, is that digital opportunities for communication have been almost completely pushed aside in the 21st century classroom. He writes:

> Social networking sites, at their core, are just aggregations of a set of Web 2.0 building blocks—forums, directories, "friending," chat, etc. Just as you can build either a casino or a school with basic construction materials, the materials are not the issue. It is the end use for which they are assembled and fitted. The first sites that were constructed using Web 2.0 building blocks were, as often as not, "casino-like," leading to the impression that social networking was a time waster at best, and an unsafe place to be at worst. But there's no reason why the same building blocks that built those social networking "casinos" can't be used to create schools, libraries, meeting halls, teachers' lounges—which is exactly what we're starting to see happening today. It is even arguable that these building blocks are more effective as educational tools than as social ones. (Hargadon, 2009, p. 2)

This chapter is designed to help teachers find ways to use social tools for communication in order to create the kinds of meaningful educational experiences that Hargadon describes. We begin with a careful look at how the four unique traits of digital conversations—persistence, searchability, replicability, and invisible audiences—are changing teen communication patterns. We also study the impact that carefully structured digital conversations can have on the social status of marginalized students and the characteristics of learning experiences that are the most motivating to iGeners.

Then we explore how Socratic circles, a centuries-old instructional practice, can bridge the gap between what students are currently doing and what we would like to see them doing online. We also introduce the differences between collaborative and competitive dialogue—communication styles that accomplished teachers systematically teach to their students whether or not they are connected—and share handouts for structuring productive synchronous and asynchronous conversations. Teachers who work through these materials will be better prepared to create electronic forums in which their students can join together with local or international peers to have Socratic-style conversations around contentious topics.

New Media Environments and iGeners

While new tools for facilitating conversations are playing an increasingly prominent role in the lives of our students, few have spent as much time studying the unique characteristics of digital communication as danah boyd, a social media researcher at Microsoft Research New England. boyd (2010), whose professional interest has always been the impact that social media is having on teens and identity, demonstrates early in her chapter of *Hanging Out, Messing Around, and Geeking Out* that iGeners value opportunities to connect online. "While these teens may see one another at school, in formal or unstructured activities, or at one another's houses," she writes, "they use social media to keep in touch with their friends, classmates, and peers when getting together is not possible. . . . For many contemporary teenagers, losing access to social media is tantamount to losing their social world" (boyd, 2010, p. 79).

Perhaps the greatest challenge facing the digitally connected teen, though, is that they are *always* plugged in. Paired with widespread access to high-speed wireless Internet connections, their mobile phones, iPods, and gaming devices extend communication in ways that were once impossible—and while most teens thrive on this newfound ability to talk at any time, there are social implications for unchecked connectivity. Online profiles must be diligently maintained or students run the risk of losing status among their peers. Messages must be returned immediately or students run the risk of offending friends. Public expressions of friendship must be significant and sincere or students run the risk of quickly becoming embroiled in social drama at school (boyd, 2010).

Complicating matters is that all of this interaction takes place in digital forums defined by four unique characteristics (boyd, 2007).

1. **Persistence:** Most electronic communication is permanent. Comments added to online discussions can be viewed days, weeks, or months later. Participants unable to be present at the time of a conversation can still see what others had to say. No one is left out of a digital conversation, and opinions expressed—whether good or bad—hang around.

2. **Searchability:** When digital conversations are recorded and names are attached to content, the thoughts and ideas of any individual become instantly searchable. With little effort, users of digital communication tools can profile peers, accessing information publicly posted over long periods of time.

3. **Replicability:** Content added to digital conversations can also be copied and pasted easily. Ideas and opinions shared spontaneously can be taken out of context and spread quickly

through email, texts, and instant messaging services, carrying long-term unintended consequences.

4. **Invisible audiences:** When communicating with traditional audiences, speakers have a good sense of who is listening and can tailor messages accordingly. Digital audiences, however, are difficult if not impossible to define. The invisible members of digital audiences—those who inadvertently stumble across public expressions—may interpret ideas differently than they were originally intended.

The persistent, searchable, and replicable nature of digital conversations held publicly in front of invisible audiences means that social gaffes can be especially costly for iGeners. Pictures and videos of inappropriate or irresponsible behavior are reposted across the Internet. Slurs and insults made in moments of frustration become public knowledge immediately. Rumors spread uncontrolled, leaving victims unprotected and socially destroyed. The structural boundaries that limit communication in traditional environments—Who is present? What did they see or hear? What can they remember? Who will they tell? What evidence do they have to share?—are nonexistent in digital forums, amplifying the consequences of communication mistakes in the 21st century (boyd, 2007).

But the same four characteristics of digital forums—persistence, searchability, replicability, and invisible audiences—can have a positive impact on students when electronic conversations become a regular part of classroom instruction. First, the transparent nature of electronic conversations provides an equalizing opportunity for students who are typically disenfranchised. Students who are socially or economically isolated or who often have academic difficulty are frequently stereotyped as nonlearners by peers and judged as uninterested by teachers. Students in these groups, however, tend to participate in electronic conversations at higher rates than they participate in traditional classroom conversations, earning intellectual recognition for perhaps the first time (Ferriter, 2005).

Students who face pressures to conform also engage in electronic conversations at higher rates than they participate in traditional classroom conversations. The potentially anonymous nature of digital dialogue serves as a safety blanket for students afraid of ridicule. Because joining in electronic conversations can be done anywhere and at any time, thoughts can be carefully crafted before they are posted. Thus, there is little risk of being embarrassed by poorly polished comments. These assurances encourage participation from students who would have sat on the sidelines in the classroom, hypersensitive to the potential negative reactions of classmates and friends (Ferriter, 2005).

Finally, electronic conversations can challenge thinking. Students who participate in digital dialogue are forced to clarify their preexisting notions as they consider alternative positions. This process of mental justification is a higher-level thinking skill and one of the strongest benefits of electronic conversations (Ferriter, 2005). What's more, students can tailor their participation in electronic conversations, following the most motivating strands or individuals. This ability to tailor participation provides a level of intellectual differentiation that is hard to find in traditionally structured classrooms. Better yet, the permanence of electronic conversations means they never lose their instructional value. Students can wrestle with new concepts or return to reflect on their initial positions whenever it is developmentally appropriate to do so.

Knowing that their students are already gathering with local peers in digital forums for communicating, accomplished teachers are working to craft school-based conversations that catch the attention of teens. The key, not surprisingly, is building forums around interesting content. Students don't automatically reject online conversations with learning-related outcomes and higher levels of adult participation. They do, however, draw clear lines between opportunities to interact informally with peers and opportunities to study topics of deep personal interest. As the researchers behind the MacArthur Foundation's Digital Youth Project concluded, "Friendship-driven and interest-driven online participation have very different kinds of social connotations . . . friendship-driven activities center on peer culture, adult participation is more welcome in the latter, more 'geeky,' forms of learning" (Ito et al., 2009, p. 2).

Digital teens are also drawn to learning experiences that allow the following (Ito et al., 2009).

- **Self-directed exploration:** In new media environments, students are surrounded by opportunities to experiment, explore without predetermined outcomes or goals in mind, and receive immediate feedback from diverse audiences.

- **Peers to demonstrate authority and expertise:** In new media environments, students regularly learn from one another, whether they are showing friends how to defeat a shared video game or are being shown tips and tricks for working with new tools. These opportunities have fundamentally changed how teens view authority and expertise.

- **Students to wrestle with meaningful issues:** Schools have traditionally been charged with preparing students for meaningful careers. As a result, instruction emphasizes the mastery of skills seen as essential for success in the workplace. In new media environments, however, students are often exposed to concepts far more complex and morally pressing. Preparing to play an active role in public conversations around these issues resonates with students.

The implications that the rapidly changing communication practices of tweens and teens hold for educators are clear. First, our students are more connected to their local peers—friends from church, teammates, neighbors—than ever before. While social media allow for communication across geographic boundaries, most teens remain primarily interested in communicating with people they already know (Ito et al., 2009), which means motivation levels for school-based conversations should be high. What's more, the persistent, searchable, and replicable nature of digital conversations can create opportunities for marginalized students to gain social status in front of their peers (Ferriter, 2005). But in order to guarantee participation, school-based conversations must revolve around meaningful content, allow students self-directed opportunities for exploration, and respect the expertise and authority of all participants.

Collaborative Versus Competitive Dialogue

The solution to ensuring that school-based conversations—whether they happen in person or online—are productive is surprisingly simple and thousands of years old: it is time for teachers to reintroduce their students to Socratic circles. Based on the thinking of the ancient Greek philosopher and teacher Socrates, Socratic circles give students the opportunity to interact with one another in conversations around shared texts connected to provocative issues. There are no predetermined outcomes or learning goals attached to Socratic circles—and the best conversations are student led. High school English teacher Matt Copeland (2005), author of *Socratic Circles: Fostering Critical and Creative Thinking in Middle and High School*, writes, "Socratic circles turn partial classroom control, classroom direction, and classroom governance over to students by creating a truly equitable learning community in which the weight and value of student voices and teacher voices are indistinguishable" (p. 3).

If you were to watch a traditional Socratic seminar in action, you would see a classroom divided into two groups: an inner circle of participants wrestling directly with the content being studied and an outer circle of silent observers tracking provocative ideas and conversation behaviors. Members of the inner circle—having read and annotated a shared text ahead of time—would work first to create meaning together. Questions would be asked, ideas would be challenged, and conclusions would be drawn. Their peers in the outer circle would then provide constructive feedback on the interactions that took place between classmates before moving into the inner circle and continuing the conversation themselves. "It is the interaction between the inner and outer circles that enables students to control the direction and process of the dialogue taking place," writes Copeland (2005, p. 9).

Throughout the seminar, the classroom teacher would be managing logistics: keeping time, allowing both groups to play the participant and observer roles, tracking patterns of interaction, summarizing key ideas, and facilitating a final discussion about both the content and the conversational strengths and weaknesses of the class. While teachers may begin inner circle conversations with focused questions and redirect student groups when discussions stall, their primary responsibility is to turn control of the dialogue over to their students. "Of course, the teacher is still nearby to take those reins back if the horses begin to run wild and out of control," writes Copeland (2005, p. 62).

Successful Socratic circles depend on teaching students the differences between collaborative and competitive dialogue. Competitive dialogue—frequently rewarded by our world—is predicated on the belief that there are winners and losers in every conversation. Companies fighting for market share, politicians fighting for votes, and celebrities fighting for attention are all modeling competitive dialogue. In competitive dialogue, everyone is an opponent instead of an ally (Copeland, 2005).

Collaborative dialogue, on the other hand, depends on a mutual desire to create shared knowledge. "One of the most prevalent misconceptions students have about Socratic circles is that they are a form of competitive debate in which participants argue to win," writes Copeland (2005). "This can be destructive to the quality of classroom dialogue, because dialogue represents the collaborative quest to construct knowledge" (p. 46). Participants in collaborative dialogue assume that everyone has good intentions, changing the way they respond to one another. Open-minded questions are asked and emphasis is placed on drawing new conclusions instead of on deciding whose initial positions were correct. Challenges are seen as pathways to new learning and participants look for strengths in the positions of others as opposed to pointing out perceived weaknesses (Copeland, 2005).

Promoting the kind of dialogue that leads to the collaborative construction of knowledge depends on introducing students to a set of specific conversation behaviors. These behaviors include working to engage silent students, making conversations safe for every participant, asking strong questions, correcting inaccurate thinking, and successfully navigating disagreements.

Working to Engage Silent Students

In many classroom conversations, there will be students who sit silently and watch the conversation go by. To the casual observer, these students may appear uninterested or unintelligent. Silent participants, however, are often actively listening and mentally engaged. They are simply intimidated by assertive peers and unwilling to elbow their way into spirited conversations.

Recognizing that multiple perspectives strengthen shared understandings, students in the most successful collaborative discussions see silent peers as missed opportunities and systematically use targeted questions to draw them into the conversation. To reinforce the importance of engaging everyone in a collaborative dialogue, teachers publicly highlight examples of successful efforts to include students who would have otherwise remained silent. They also stress that silent students have a responsibility to lend their voices to shared conversations, painting inaction as a behavior that carries intellectual costs for everyone.

Making Conversations Safe for Every Participant

In many classroom conversations, a small handful of students end up dominating the course of a discussion. Making frequent comments focused on areas of personal interest, they ignore the contributions of others and jump in anytime there is a moment of free space that no one else is filling. To the casual observer, it seems like these students are talking to themselves!

Changing this behavior starts with careful conversation tracking by both teachers and students. Assertive students must be able to visually see that their involvement limits the opportunities for others to get involved. Assertive students should also be taught to ask open-ended questions, to elicit thinking from other peers, and to build on strands of conversation that have already been started. Teachers should highlight places where the work of an otherwise dominant participant brought new ideas to the collective table.

Asking Strong Questions

The collaborative construction of shared knowledge depends on one key ingredient: strong questions. Strong questions hook participants, encouraging them to share. Strong questions challenge peers to think differently, lead conversations in new directions, and leave room for other participants. Sometimes strong questions are asked of the entire group. Sometimes strong questions are asked of individual members. Regardless, strong conversations cannot happen without someone who is willing to ask the kinds of questions that make other people think.

Encouraging students to question begins by spotlighting the most provocative and challenging ideas added to each conversation. Celebrating questions reminds students that effective contributions to ongoing conversations are not always statements of opinions or facts. While working in the outer circle of a Socratic seminar, teachers can ask students to record motivating questions and extend strands of thinking when they become members of the inner circle. Strong questions can also be revisited during follow-up conversations, posted in classroom collections, or become the focus of new studies.

Correcting Inaccurate Thinking

Regardless of how carefully students have studied a topic, inaccurate information is bound to be shared during the course of any collaborative conversation. Students who share inaccurate information are not intentionally trying to confuse their peers, they just don't know as much about the subject of the conversation as they think they do. Seeing correction as a form of disrespect, however, most students allow inaccuracies shared during Socratic circles to go unchallenged.

Working to change this behavior depends on helping students understand that correcting peers isn't inherently disrespectful. Instead, when handled with careful language and in the context of a collaborative effort to build shared understanding, it can be an intentional attempt to help someone grow as a learner. Challenging inaccuracies is best done by presenting direct evidence—the text being studied, previous lessons, independent learning experiences—of competing perspectives. Doing so encourages students making inaccurate statements to mentally wrestle with ideas that they once held to be true.

Successfully Navigating Disagreements

Good conversations are bound to have moments of open disagreement between participants. In fact, conversations *without* disagreement are typically evidence of poorly selected topics or poorly prepared students. Conversations in which everyone agrees also tend to be the least motivating to 21st century students who want to wrestle with provocative ideas together. The challenge with competing viewpoints in Socratic circles, however, is that students are taught from an early age that polite participation in classroom activities means avoiding disagreements.

For collaborative conversations to result in new learning, students need to be encouraged to embrace intellectual discord as an opportunity to polish and refine collective thinking. Reaching the point where an open-minded approach to disagreement is possible depends on teaching students to trust the intentions of their peers. When thinkers in a Socratic circle believe that everyone is working toward the same end goal—to learn together—it is possible to disagree with an idea instead of an individual. You should also teach students to use specific words or phrases when expressing disagreement and to publicly share times when their thinking has been changed by peers. Making the successful outcomes of disagreement transparent lends a sense of safety to collaborative conversations around controversial topics.

Accomplished teachers recognize that the content outcomes of collaborative conversations are only possible when students are skilled communicators. As a result, they design frequent opportunities for their students to observe and evaluate the dialogue behaviors of their peers. A handout that students can use to track contributions to classroom conversations can be found on page 112.

Digital Opportunities to Connect

Socratic circles resonate with iGeners primarily because they align so well with the characteristics of the digital worlds that our students inhabit beyond school. Questions from peers provide the most significant challenge in the best Socratic circles. Authority and control over the direction of inquiry rests in the hands of participants in Socratic circles. Socratic circles are defined by collective exploration and collaboration around meaningful problems.

The best news is that translating Socratic practices to the kinds of online conversations that our students are already having is easy when using new media tools for communication. Software applications such as Edmodo (www.edmodo.com) allow teachers to create ongoing, asynchronous digital forums focused on topics studied in class. In addition, classes are participating in synchronous discussions using applications such as Skype (www.skype.com) and Google Hangouts (www.google.com/hangouts). Some teachers are also using microblogging applications such as Twitter (www.twitter.com) to extend classroom conversations around interesting content.

Classrooms across the United States are even finding ways to enhance their in-school Socratic circles with synchronous and asynchronous learning tools. Chat applications like TodaysMeet (https://todaysmeet.com) allow students in the outer circle to instantly interact around the information being shared by the inner circle. Facilitators can encourage students in the outer circle to use the web to confirm the information being shared in the inner circle. This process allows all students to be engaged in the learning process and provides opportunities for collaborative dialogue that builds meaning.

For students, access to digital conversations around school-based content—whether they take place at home or in school—is unexpectedly motivating. Evidence of that motivation can be found in the following quotes, collected from a 2008 survey of sixth-grade students who used VoiceThread (http://voicethread.com), a free tool for facilitating asynchronous conversations, over the course of an entire year to extend Socratic circles started in their language arts and social studies classrooms (Ferriter, 2008):

> VoiceThread allows me to hear the thoughts of many other students just like me! I can think differently about the same topic, and people really do challenge my mind. I also like to respond to people and challenge their thinking and share the way I think with them.

Commenting, arguing, discussing, and agreeing on many different topics . . . is very fun. Although, sharing your views about things and having people respond is the best thing about VoiceThread!

I really enjoy VoiceThread because it is a cool way to have a digi-conversation with people from your class. . . . Several new ideas that I wouldn't have thought of bounce around my head after I visit VoiceThread. It is something new every day.

The reason why I like our VoiceThread . . . is because it gives you a chance to communicate with people online and also you get to see their opinion. . . . Personally I hate ending conversations because you never know if something is going to pop into your mind.

While synchronous and asynchronous opportunities to connect are equally motivating to students and provide similar opportunities for practicing collaborative dialogue, each requires teachers to follow a unique set of instructional steps.

Asynchronous Conversations

Instructionally, structuring asynchronous conversations that motivate your students depends on the careful selection of content. The best asynchronous forums are often extensions of in-class Socratic circles. Along with introductory comments sharing simple conversation reminders and directions, post the quotes, questions, and ideas that sparked animated thinking in your inner and outer circles before opening digital discussions to your students. When you are ready to introduce your digital discussion to your classes, encourage students to carefully preview the developing conversation by using the "Previewing an Asynchronous Conversation" handout found on page 113. Asking students to track their initial thinking before adding posts to your digital seminar can help ensure that all contributions are meaningful and interesting.

Remember that your role in asynchronous forums should mirror the role that teachers play in traditional Socratic circles. You are there to support students, not to control conversations. Ask provocative questions to stimulate stalled conversations, model proper discussion language, spotlight particularly original thoughts in class, use selected contributions as extensions in lessons, and help students identify motivating strands of conversation to join. For the duration of an asynchronous conversation, create a borderless learning experience in which the thinking done online spurs discussions in your classroom and the thinking done in class spurs productive contributions to the intellectual collaboration taking place online.

In classes struggling with the kinds of behaviors that support collaborative dialogue, it can be helpful to introduce students to a series of specific comment types and templates that encourage healthy contributions to asynchronous discussions. These comment types—described for students in the handout "Commenting in an Asynchronous Conversation" (page 114)—can include the following.

- **Starter comments:** Sometimes students will add new content such as questions, statistics, images, videos, and quotes to an asynchronous conversation. Each new piece of content must be paired with a starter comment that focuses the thinking of other participants. Starter comments can introduce the source for new content, the connections between new content and the existing conversation, or a position statement explaining how a student feels about the new content he or she has brought to a digital conversation.

- **Kicker comments:** Sometimes students will be the first to add thoughts to a thread started by another participant. These types of comments are called kicker comments because they "kick off" a strand of conversation. Students making kicker comments should begin by responding to questions asked by the user who posted the original content. Students making kicker comments should then explain their own thinking—backing assertions with evidence, connecting to ideas shared in class, and supporting or disagreeing with the ideas of others. Finally, students making kicker comments should finish with interesting, open-ended questions that encourage others to speak up.

- **Pushback comments:** Sometimes students will agree and want to add more elaboration to support a central point, or they may disagree and want to challenge the thinking of their peers. These kinds of comments are called pushbacks. Pushback comments must begin with a quote from the thinking to be supported or challenged and must include enough elaboration to allow others to easily follow the direction of the conversation.

- **Answering comments:** Sometimes students will want to answer a question leveled directly at them or asked of the entire group. In many ways, responding to questions is the lifeblood of collaborative dialogue, because such responses let participants know that their ideas are valuable and interesting to others. Thoughtfully responding to questions encourages participation and keeps digital conversations moving forward. Answering comments should begin with the question that was asked, include a thorough answer, and ask follow-up questions whenever possible.

It can also be helpful to share sample strands of discussion with students when structuring asynchronous learning opportunities. Sample strands serve as de facto role plays of digital conversations, allowing students to explore the characteristics of positive interactions, see the language of digital dialogue modeled, and pinpoint the kinds of behaviors that cripple online conversations. While the most effective sample strands of conversation will always be those drawn from the work done in your own classroom, an initial reflection sheet, "What Can Digital Conversations Look Like?," can be found on page 116. Finally, developing effective asynchronous conversation skills depends on providing students with meaningful feedback. After completing an online conversation, ask students to use the "Reflecting on an Asynchronous Conversation" handout (page 119) to record how their own thinking changed as a result of the contributions that others made to your discussion and the "Scoring Student Participation in Asynchronous Conversations" rubric (page 120) to rate the contributions of one of their peers. Doing so will create a classroom environment in which effective digital communication is an expectation that students are willing to hold themselves—and one another—accountable for.

Technically, the asynchronous conversation process starts with selecting a service for hosting digital discussions. While there will always be dozens of services to choose from, the basic features that you should consider before making a final decision will always remain the same.

- **Simultaneous strands of conversation:** The best digital conversations allow students to target their participation by focusing on the ideas that are the most individually motivating. As a result, good forums for digital communication allow users to create and maintain several different strands of conversation related to the same topic at the same time.

- **Control of conversation privacy settings:** In the most progressive classrooms, conversations around controversial topics are open for public viewing and participation, which provides an audience for student ideas and a source for new challenges to the fundamental beliefs developed during the course of digital discussions. Sometimes, however, district policies prohibit this kind of transparent work online, requiring classroom conversations to be closed to public viewing. Any application that you choose for digital conversations must allow you to tailor privacy settings.

- **Interaction around a wide range of content types:** Students are increasingly motivated by multimedia content. Most early asynchronous conversation tools are text-based, which can be inherently dissatisfying to teens used to websites that regularly incorporate streaming audio and video. Selecting applications that allow students to both consume and produce video and audio content in asynchronous conversations can help ensure that motivation levels in your classroom remain high.

- **The ability to search and archive any conversation:** As your students become more adept at interacting with one another in digital forums, you will not only find that the conversations they engage in will become powerful examples of collaborative thought, but also that the content generated can be used to promote continued reflection long after a conversation ends. Ensuring that each conversation becomes a long-term learning tool depends on selecting a service that allows users to search within conversations as well as archive them once they end.

One of the best free tools available to teachers interested in asynchronous conversations is VoiceThread (http://ed.voicethread.com), mentioned earlier. Teachers and students can upload video clips, images, documents, charts, graphs, and PowerPoint presentations to start individual strands of conversation. What's more, text, audio, and video comments can be added to VoiceThread conversations, lending a sense of interactivity and personality that is often missing in asynchronous conversations. To see what VoiceThread conversations can look like in action, explore the samples introduced in the "VoiceThread in Action" handout found on page 121.

After selecting a service to host your asynchronous conversations, you will need to think through a wide range of other technical considerations. You will need to consult with your school and district technology services departments to make sure you are following any procedures or protocols that have already been established for asynchronous conversations. Carefully choose your privacy settings for these digital discussions to ensure that your students are safe while working online. Also, experiment with the asynchronous application you have chosen to be sure that it is accessible behind your district's firewall and that it functions well on the computers your students have access to. The "Asynchronous Conversation Checklist" (page 123) can help you effectively prepare for successful asynchronous conversations.

Synchronous Opportunities to Connect

While asynchronous discussions between peers who know one another offline neatly aligns with the ways in which new media environments are already being used by your students, limiting digital conversations to local peers overlooks the very real potential to develop the kinds of cross-border relationships and understandings that Tim Berners-Lee imagined when first designing the Internet. The most accomplished teachers are moving beyond asynchronous conversations between classmates to *synchronous* conversations that connect their students to classes in other countries, because they recognize that exposure to international peers means exposure to multiple perspectives on the critical issues that pose challenges worldwide, such as poverty, global warming, drought, wars, deforestation, and immigration. These experiences, argues Don Tapscott (2009) in *Grown Up Digital*, are essential to developing the kinds of globally aware and active citizens that our world needs in order to survive:

> Will their civic activity around the world become a new kind of activism? Will they rise to the challenges of deepening problems that my generation is handing them? Never has there been a time of greater promise or peril. The challenge of achieving that promise and in so doing saving our fragile planet will rest with the Net Generation. Our responsibility to them is to give them the tools and the opportunity to fulfill their destiny. (Kindle location 851–855)

Giving your students the tools to fulfill Tapscott's vision of global activism begins by selecting an application for hosting synchronous conversations. In most cases, this decision begins by having a conversation with your school or district's technology services specialists. Unlike the web-based tools used for asynchronous conversations, which generally place few demands on a school's digital resources, tools for synchronous conversations can stretch a network's capability to capacity. As a result, many districts carefully monitor the synchronous communication in their schools, defining specific procedures that must be followed when connecting with classes in real-time and supporting specific services for conducting these kinds of conversations. Also, many school districts have built familiar social media tools into their learning management systems in order to ensure that all communications can be monitored. Working carefully with your technology services department can guarantee that you are not confronted with any digital surprises during synchronous conversations.

Once you have been given permission to conduct synchronous conversations, you will need to think through a wide range of additional technical questions. Will your students need individual accounts to use the service that you have selected? If so, how will those accounts be created? Are you planning to record and archive each synchronous conversation? If so, where will the archived recordings be posted? Does your school have a quiet room that can be set aside for classroom videoconferencing? If so, how can you make sure that students working with international peers are uninterrupted during the course of their conversations? Planning questions like these can be found on the "Teacher Videoconferencing Checklist" (page 126).

Giving students the opportunity to fulfill Tapscott's vision of global activism also depends on finding classes to partner with—perhaps the most intimidating challenge for teachers new to digital learning experiences. The good news is that you are not the only teacher interested in pairing your classes with peers abroad. Companies like ePals (www.epals.com) have been connecting classrooms globally for years and have expanded to provide social media tools to enhance communication. Skype has also developed a home for educators interested in finding national or international partners for their classes (https://education.skype.com) that can be searched by grade level, subject area, and country.

As you work to select classes to connect with, prioritize the topic of the conversation you are planning. If you are studying global poverty, for example, look for classes in the developing world that can provide firsthand accounts of life in poor nations or classes in social welfare states that take completely different national approaches to wealth and social justice. Finding potential synchronous conversation partners with competing viewpoints and experiences will add the mental tension and intellectual discord that drive motivating discussions and real learning. Poor choices at this stage—selecting partners in nations whose approaches and perspectives mirror those in your own country—will limit the learning outcomes of the digital conversations that you are working so hard to structure.

Preparing students for synchronous conversations requires more than simply making good choices when selecting sister schools, however. Much like the skills necessary for effective participation in Socratic circles and asynchronous conversations, students engaged in real-time discussions with classes in other countries must be ready to have their own thinking challenged and to challenge the thinking of their global peers. They must also see synchronous videoconferences as an opportunity to think together. Finally, they must be willing to approach every synchronous conversation with an open mind and a willingness to change their preconceived notions about the topic being studied based on information collected from international peers.

The "Tracking Your Videoconference" handout—found on page 128 and designed to walk students through a set of structured pre-, during-, and post-videoconference questions—can help your classes make the most of synchronous conversations.

Final Thoughts

For twelve-year-old Tommy, science was the best class of the school day because it never seemed to end. Not only did he have hands-on experiences with light, sound, and heat to look forward to, but he also had ongoing asynchronous conversations to engage in once he'd gotten home. Together with his classmates, he was involved in an ongoing cycle of scientific thought that started during second period and ended just before bedtime. In animated conversations before class, during lunch, around their lockers, and online, Tommy and his likeminded peers spent time designing original experiments, testing hypotheses, sharing observations, drawing conclusions, and asking new questions. "I love educational subjects," said Tommy, "and now that I had a message board with science as its topic, I had the message board that I liked. It was very fun to talk to other people online and discuss the subjects we were studying in class" (T. Pendleton, personal communication, May 27, 2004).

Tommy, a quiet boy who had moved to the United States in the middle of the school year and initially had trouble fitting in, quickly became a digital star. The questions he asked made others think differently and kept them coming back for more. His creativity made others imagine. Dozens of new experiments—conducted both at home and in the classroom—were born from strands started by Tommy in asynchronous conversations. For Tommy, the digital opportunities to communicate created by his teacher encouraged students to spend more time thinking about school. "They go to school, they do their homework, and then log on—so they spend more time learning than if they just went to school and then did their homework," he argued (T. Pendleton, personal communication, May 27, 2004).

Through it all, Tommy and his peers felt in charge, studying interesting questions simply because they could. That same sense of student-driven discovery can become a part of the intellectual life of your classroom if you are willing to create opportunities—both online and in school—for collaborative dialogue between peers.

Curriculum Matters: The Common Core State Standards

According to the Speaking and Listening Strand of the Common Core State Standards, students must be able to "engage effectively in a range of collaborative discussions" (NGA & CCSSO, 2010). This means that students should come to conversations prepared to express their own ideas clearly, build on ideas shared by others, demonstrate an understanding of multiple perspectives, and ask and answer specific questions with elaboration and detail (NGA & CCSSO, 2010).

Do these skills also appear in the curricula for your classes? Are they skills that you believe are important for iGeners? Which activities, strategies, and tools presented in this chapter would help students master these skills?

Tracking Conversation Behaviors

Productive classroom conversations depend on our ability to engage silent students, make conversations safe for every participant, ask good questions, correct inaccurate thinking, and successfully navigate disagreements. Use this handout to spot these behaviors during our classroom conversations.

Discussion Behavior	Your Response
Engaging silent students: To get every good idea into our conversation, it is important to hear from everyone in our discussion. As you watch our conversation, record students who do a good job engaging silent students. What impact do these attempts have on our conversation?	
Making conversations safe for every student: Sometimes conversations are taken over by one or two students who talk so much that other students can't get involved. As you watch our conversation, record instances where this happens. What impact do these behaviors have on our conversation?	
Working to ask good questions: Good questions are essential to healthy conversations because they start new strands of discussion and challenge thinking. As you watch our conversation, record the best questions that are asked. What impact do these questions have on our conversation?	
Working to correct inaccurate thinking: Sometimes students will share ideas in our conversation that are inaccurate. To make our conversation meaningful, these inaccurate ideas have to be corrected. As you watch our conversation, record moments where inaccurate ideas *are not* corrected. What impact does this flawed thinking have on our conversation?	
Working through disagreements: In the best conversations, participants who disagree will work to understand—rather than argue—with one another. As you watch our conversation, record moments where participants who disagree with one another end up in an argument. What impact does their disagreement have on our conversation?	

Previewing an Asynchronous Conversation

Title of Presentation:

While previewing this asynchronous conversation, track your thinking on this handout. Remember that good participants in digital conversations are always asking questions, making connections, forming opinions, and gathering facts. Be sure to note specific places where you'd like to add comments or respond to other viewers. Consider starting your comments with phrases like: *I notice, I wonder, I realized, You can relate this to, Although it seems, This reminds me of, I'm not sure that,* and *If I were _____, I would _____.*

Thread Title:

Content Description

What key points are expressed in the content of this thread? In the comments added by your peers?

Your Initial Thoughts

What ideas do you agree with here? Disagree with? What new directions would you like to take this conversation in?

Possible Comments

Write a draft of a potential comment here. Remember to use the computer to polish any text comments that you add to our conversation.

Questions for Reflection

1. Do you agree with the general direction that this conversation is heading in? Why or why not? What key points are being left out that you intend to bring to the digital table?

2. What connections can you make between this conversation and content that you have studied in other places and at other times? How can you integrate those connections into this conversation?

3. Which strand of conversation is the most motivating to you? Why? When will you return to see how that strand of conversation is developing?

Commenting in an Asynchronous Conversation

Title of Presentation:

Over the next several days, we'll continue the conversation that we started in our last Socratic circle online. Use this handout to script any comments that you plan to add to our digital discussion. Remember that scripting comments will help you post ideas that are easy to understand. Also remember that if you plan to add text comments, you should proofread for spelling and grammar errors.

Starter Comments

Sometimes you will add new content (threads, images, quotes, video) to an asynchronous conversation. When you do, it is important to include a starter comment to focus the thinking of other participants.

The following sentence stems will help you structure starter comments for new content that you add to our asynchronous conversation.

- What do you notice about this _____ titled _____ and showing _____?

- This _____ really resonates with me because _____. It makes me think _____. Does anyone else feel the same way?

- When we were talking about this _____ in our classroom conversation, it made me feel _____. How did it make you feel?

Kicker Comments

Sometimes, you will find that you are the first person to add comments to content added by someone else in our asynchronous conversation—or you might have a completely original idea that no one else has brought up yet. These types of comments are called kicker comments because they "kick off" a new strand of conversation. When making a kicker comment, it is important to remember to respond to any questions asked by the user who posted the original content. It is also important to finish kicker comments with interesting questions that will encourage other viewers to speak up.

The following sentence stems will help you structure interesting kicker comments.

- I noticed _____

- This was interesting to me because _____

Pushback Comments

Sometimes, you will want to respond to something that another participant said in our asynchronous conversation. You may agree and want to add more elaboration. You may disagree and want to challenge their thinking. These kinds of comments are called pushbacks. In a pushback comment, it is important to quote the person you are responding to so that other participants will know what caught your attention. It is also important to elaborate on your point of view and to disagree agreeably! Impolite people are never influential.

Teaching the iGeneration © 2010, 2015 Solution Tree Press • solution-tree.com
Visit **go.solution-tree.com/technology** or **plugusin.pbworks.com** to download this page.

The following sentence stems will help you structure interesting pushback comments:

- _____ said _____.
- I (agree/disagree) with (him/her) because _____.
- I think that _____.
- I am wondering if _____.

Answering Comments

Sometimes, you will want to answer a question that another commenter asked in an asynchronous conversation. Their question may have been directed right to you, or it may have been asked to the group as a whole. Responding to questions is incredibly important because it lets others know that their ideas are valuable and interesting. Responding to questions moves asynchronous conversations forward and keeps them interesting.

The following sentence stems will help you structure interesting answering comments:

- _____ asked _____. This is a really interesting question, _____.
- I think _____.
- I also think _____.
- Do you agree with me on _____? Looking forward to your reply!

What Can Digital Conversations Look Like?

A group of middle school students using pseudonyms extended a Socratic circle on hatred by having an asynchronous conversation together on VoiceThread (http://ed.voicethread.com/hare/88781). Use this handout to study one strand from that conversation, in which students reflected on a quote from their original seminar.

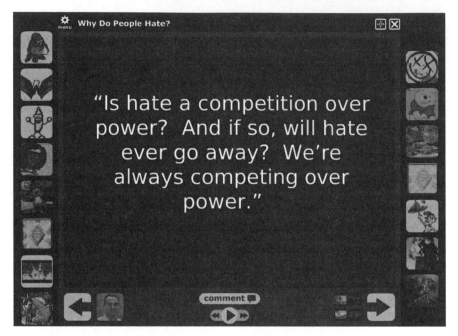

Source: VoiceThread. Used with permission.

Student Conversation
Darth Tater: Here's an interesting quote on hatred that came from a seminar on hatred in my classroom. What do you think the connections are between hatred and power? Do hatred and a quest for power go hand in hand?
Evil Barney: I think that the quest for power just sets the stage for hatred to occur. Whenever I play the game Risk, I notice that I become frustrated with other players that stop my conquest. I bet when people are trying to gain power on a large scale in real life, that frustration builds up like lava in a volcano and comes out as violence and hate all at once. I don't think power is completely to blame for hatred, but it definitely helps hatred come along. What else do you think power does for hatred?
Mearan: Hate, most of the time, is competing over power. For example, you are nominated for president. Then, another candidate wins the election. You are not going to be very happy are you? You will end up generating hate toward that person, even if it is only a small bit. Now, hate cannot be stopped, for it is a natural human emotion. As I have said before "we could create the illusion of it disappearing, but it will never be true." Saying that, we could lessen people's will to be in a higher power. It could lessen the hate, but it would never go away. Is there any way to eliminate the humans need to be at the top of power?

Student Conversation
The Happy Man: Mearan said: Is there any way to eliminate the humans need to be at the top of power? My answer is that there really isn't. The only thing we can do is either get rid of that power or make power a little less glamorous. Most likely, neither of those things is going to happen. The most anyone can do is wait for something to happen that does eliminate that need. But in the grand scheme of things, is there really any need for one person to have all that power?
Pooh Bear: Evil Barney said: "I think that the quest for power just sets the stage for hatred to occur." This really grabs my attention. Everyone keeps on saying that hate is expressed because of power. But what Evil Barney says is that power is kind of a step up to get to hatred. It leads to hatred . . . When you feel power or the more you want it, it forces your hate to come out even stronger. A lot of the time in life, for some reason, people want to be powerful. I don't understand. What is the significance of this? Why is control such an exciting word to people? It is kind of like an evil scientist or somebody in a movie. You might gain something so great, and so wanted by other people, that it can get out of hand. By people wanting that thing (power) so much, you feel hate toward them because they want the power that you have and don't want to be taken away. So I guess my overall question is: Why do people love the feeling of power and control?
Mearan: Evil Barney said: "I think that the quest for power just sets the stage for hatred to occur," and Pooh Bear said: "Power is kind of a step up to get to hatred. It leads to hatred." I somewhat agree with this. However, I see power as more of a fuel. Let's think of hate as fire. The more the quest for power occurs, the more fuel you will have. So, if you have lots of fuel and then light the flames of hatred, the flame will be big. Depending on the amount of fuel you had at the start, the flames of hatred will last longer, or it will be bigger. So a quick clap for your new way of thinking. Anyone else see this from a different viewpoint?

Questions for Reflection

1. What types of conversation comments (starter, kicker, pushback, answering) can you find in this sample strand of collaborative dialogue?

2. If you were to rank these comments in order from the most important to the least important, what would your rankings look like? Why?

3. If you were to improve one of these comments, which would you choose? What revisions would you make?

4. If you were to join this conversation, what type of comment would you add? Where would you place it?

5. Which participant do you think made the most significant contributions to this sample strand of comments? Which made the least significant contributions? Explain your thinking.

Reflecting on an Asynchronous Conversation

After a digital conversation has run its course, it is important for you to think back on what you have learned. The following four questions can serve both as a reflection guide and as evidence that you have engaged in a meaningful way with the topic we're studying together.

1. Highlight a comment from our recent conversation that closely matches your own thinking. Why does this comment resonate with—or make sense to—you?

2. Highlight a comment from our recent conversation that you respectfully disagree with. If you were to engage in a conversation with the commenter, what evidence or argument would you use to persuade him or her to change his or her point of view?

3. Highlight a comment from our recent conversation that challenged your thinking in a good way or made you rethink one of your original ideas. What about the new comment was challenging? What are you going to do now that your original belief was challenged? Will you change your mind? Do more researching, thinking, or talking with others?

4. Highlight the strand of conversation from our recent conversation that was the most interesting or motivating to you. Which ideas would you like to have more time to talk about? Why? What new topics does this conversation make you want to study next?

Scoring Student Participation in Asynchronous Conversations

Like any new skill, students need to get regular feedback in order to become stronger participants in asynchronous conversations. This rubric is designed to help teachers and students rate participation in the asynchronous conversations that we have in class.

Above Average
■ The comments you have added to our asynchronous conversation are all clearly connected to the topic we are studying.
■ Because you knew so much about our topic, you raised points that no one else had considered. Almost everything you wrote made me want to learn more.
■ You started some of the most active strands in our conversation—and your comments always made me want to respond! I found myself arguing with your points of view, answering your questions, and thinking harder each time I came across one of your comments.
■ You always seemed to find a way to respond to others. I liked that you asked and answered questions and pushed back against the thinking of others.
■ I felt like you wanted to learn as much as you wanted to teach in our conversation and that you respected the viewpoints that others brought to the table.
■ I'm really glad you were participating in our conversation because I learned so much from you—and from the people who were responding to you!

Average
■ The comments you have added to our asynchronous conversation are all connected to the topic that we are studying, but in many places they seem simple.
■ While one or two of your ideas made me think about our topic in new ways, most of the time it seemed like you weren't adding anything new to our conversation.
■ I liked that you were asking questions, but the questions you asked could all be answered easily and rarely started new strands of thinking.
■ I'm not sure that I saw you answer any questions in our conversation—even when others asked you something directly.
■ With a bit more effort to share original thoughts and to get others involved, your comments will change minds!

Needs Improvement
■ The comments you added to our conversation seemed unconnected to the topic we were studying.
■ You didn't bring many new ideas to our discussion—and that's surprising because you have good ideas to share.
■ You posted your own thinking, but I didn't see you reply to anyone. I wanted to see you push against the ideas of your classmates, ask questions, and start new strands for us to consider.

VoiceThread in Action

One of the most popular tools for asynchronous conversations is VoiceThread, a group audio blog that allows users to add text, audio, and video comments to slides containing a wide range of multimedia content. To see what VoiceThread can look like in action, spend a few minutes exploring the following conversations, which were all created by a sixth-grade language arts teacher extending traditional Socratic circles beyond the classroom.

Genocide in Darfur

http://ed.voicethread.com/share/62276

In the spring of 2007, a group of middle grade students in Massachusetts, Maryland, Virginia, and North Carolina joined together to raise attention about the genocide occurring in Darfur—a region of the African nation of Sudan. Along with blog entries and wikis designed to explain genocide to their peers, these students wrestled with the world's responsibility to help challenged nations in this VoiceThread discussion, which used political cartoons to start provocative strands of conversation.

Why Do People Hate?

http://ed.voicethread.com/share/88781

In the fall of 2008, two language arts teachers—one working with sixth graders and the other working with eighth graders—brought their students together for a Socratic circle focused on the concept of hate. For the sixth graders, this conversation was an extension of their study of the Holocaust. For the eighth graders, this conversation was an extension of their studies around the theme of justice and injustice. This VoiceThread gave both groups of students the opportunity to interact with one another before and after the traditional Socratic circle was held at school.

Learning About Adaptation and Mutation

http://ed.voicethread.com/share/518424

In the spring of 2009, a sixth-grade science teacher had his students use Flip Video camcorders to create short papercraft videos designed to introduce the concepts of natural selection, adaptation, and mutation to their peers. Then, he uploaded each group's final product to VoiceThread and asked classmates to provide one another with feedback about the overall quality of the videos produced. Doing so gave students the opportunity to practice giving and receiving constructive criticism.

Questions for Reflection

1. Is there evidence of meaningful conversation between students in these VoiceThread samples? What was surprising about the conversations that developed here? Were you impressed by anything that you saw, or is this the kind of work that you would expect from students engaged in asynchronous conversations around school-based topics?

Teaching the iGeneration © 2010, 2015 Solution Tree Press • solution-tree.com
Visit **go.solution-tree.com/technology** or **plugusin.pbworks.com** to download this page.

2. What weaknesses do you see in the conversations that developed between students in these VoiceThread samples? What conversation skills are these groups of students still struggling to master? How would you go about strengthening those weaknesses in your classroom?

3. Could your students pull off this kind of conversation with one another? What do you think it would take to get them to translate their classroom conversations into online forums? What skills would they need to learn first? When will you start teaching those skills?

4. What ideas will you steal from these VoiceThread samples to use in your own work with students? Do the format and content of any of these conversations resonate with you or meet elements of your required curriculum? Which conversation would your students be drawn to? How would you change one of these conversations to make it more appropriate, interesting, or motivating for the students in your classroom?

Teaching the iGeneration © 2010, 2015 Solution Tree Press • solution-tree.com
Visit **go.solution-tree.com/technology** or **plugusin.pbworks.com** to download this page.

Asynchronous Conversation Checklist

Asynchronous conversations provide teachers with approachable ways to extend Socratic circles and provide students with opportunities to engage with classroom content beyond the school day. This preparation checklist will help you structure successful asynchronous learning experiences for your students.

Technical and Procedural Preparations

1. Have you checked with your school or district's technology specialists to ensure that your school's Internet connection can successfully handle the demands of asynchronous conversations?

   Your Response / Next Steps:

2. Have you checked with your school or district's technology specialists to see if there are any asynchronous conversation services that they suggest or support?

   Your Response / Next Steps:

3. Have you checked with your school or district's technology specialists to see if they have any specific policies or procedures regarding student participation in asynchronous conversations?

   Your Response / Next Steps:

4. Have you experimented with the asynchronous conversation service that you plan to use to see if it is accessible at school? Are you certain that it will run effectively on the computers that your students have access to?

   Your Response / Next Steps:

5. Have you thought through the privacy settings that you plan to use for your asynchronous conversations? If you intend to make your conversations public, are you sure that you are following the Internet safety protocols required by your school or district?

   Your Response / Next Steps:

6. Have you mastered the basic skills necessary to add content and comments to conversations in the asynchronous application that you plan to use with your students? Will you be able to introduce these skills to your students?

   Your Response / Next Steps:

7. When will your students add new content or comments to your asynchronous conversations? Are you expecting them to work primarily from home on this project? Will your students need access to external devices—microphones, video cameras—to add comments to your conversations? If so, how will they access these devices?

   Your Response / Next Steps:

8. Have you set aside time to introduce students to the basic features of the digital application that you have chosen to use for asynchronous conversations? Will you train students to serve as digital mentors for their peers?

   Your Response / Next Steps:

Pedagogical Preparations

1. Are you planning on using asynchronous conversations to extend Socratic circles started in your classroom? If so, when will these Socratic circles take place? How will you choose content for the online conversation once your Socratic circle ends?

   Your Response / Next Steps:

Teaching the iGeneration © 2010, 2015 Solution Tree Press • solution-tree.com
Visit **go.solution-tree.com/technology** or **plugusin.pbworks.com** to download this page.

2. Do your students understand the kinds of discussion behaviors found in collaborative conversations? Have they had a chance to engage in collaborative conversations in class? Which behaviors do they struggle with?

   Your Response / Next Steps:

3. Are your students comfortable with the language of collaborative dialogue? If not, will you introduce several sample strands of conversation for students to explore? Is it important to introduce your students to the types of comments that users add to collaborative conversations?

   Your Response / Next Steps:

4. Do your students have enough background knowledge to be effective participants in your asynchronous conversation? How will you support their continued exploration of the topic you are studying?

   Your Response / Next Steps:

5. Have you worked out a system for spotlighting the work being done in your digital conversations? Will you spend a few minutes each day highlighting individual contributions and interactions?

   Your Response / Next Steps:

6. Have you created handouts to structure student thinking before, during, and after your asynchronous conversation?

   Your Response / Next Steps:

Teaching the iGeneration © 2010, 2015 Solution Tree Press • solution-tree.com
Visit **go.solution-tree.com/technology** or **plugusin.pbworks.com** to download this page.

Teacher Videoconferencing Checklist

With a bit of digital moxie, any teacher can facilitate synchronous conversations between classes on different continents or bring recognized experts into their rooms for synchronous conversations. This preparation checklist will help you structure successful experiences for your students.

Technical and Procedural Preparations

1. Have you checked with your school or district's technology services specialists to ensure that your school's Internet connection can successfully handle the demands of a synchronous videoconference?

   Your Response / Next Steps:

2. If you are planning on bringing a digital guest speaker into your classroom, have you checked with your principal and followed your school or district policies for using guest speakers in lessons?

   Your Response / Next Steps:

3. If you are planning on allowing groups of students to conference with peers or experts, have you found a quiet location with an Internet connection for synchronous conversations to take place?

   Your Response / Next Steps:

Pedagogical Preparations

1. If your students are working in small groups to conference with peers or experts, have you introduced them to the videoconferencing application that you are planning to use?

   Your Response / Next Steps:

2. If your students are working in small groups to conference with peers or experts, do your students have enough technical skill to deal with potential digital disasters—webcams dying, connections dropping, audio feeds failing?

    Your Response / Next Steps:

3. If your students are working in small groups to conference with peers or experts, have you worked out a schedule for individual conferences?

    Your Response / Next Steps:

4. Have you considered training a small cadre of student technology leaders to facilitate videoconferences for their peers?

    Your Response / Next Steps:

5. Do your students have enough background knowledge on the topic of your videoconference to be effective participants?

    Your Response / Next Steps:

6. Have you created handouts to structure student thinking before, during, and after your classroom videoconference?

    Your Response / Next Steps:

7. Have you developed a plan for allowing students to debrief and process what they've learned once your videoconference has ended?

    Your Response / Next Steps:

Tracking Your Videoconference

Use the following handout to guide your thinking before, during, and after your upcoming videoconference in order to be sure that connecting with digital guests is a meaningful learning experience that we can be proud of. Use the first set of questions to prepare your thinking before your videoconference even begins. Use the final set of questions to debrief after your videoconference is over.

Before Your Conference

1. List everything that you already know about your digital guests—their age, their experiences with our topic of study, the conditions in their state or country, ideas they have already shared about our topic of study, and so on.

2. Based on what you know about your digital guests, how do you think they are likely to feel about our topic of study?

3. Do you think you are likely to agree with your digital guests during your videoconference? What thoughts, ideas, and opinions are you likely to share?

4. Are you expecting there to be any sources of disagreement between your thinking and the thinking of your digital guests on the topic we are studying? What are they? Why are you likely to disagree?

5. What points do you really want to get across in the course of your digital conversation? What ideas connected to our topic of study are the most important for participants to wrestle with?

During Your Conference

1. What comments have your digital guests made that resonate with your own thinking about our topic of study? What is it about these comments that ring true for you?

2. Can you expand on the thoughts that you and your digital guests share in common? Do you have any additional facts or opinions that connect to the key ideas you agree on?

3. Have your digital guests made any comments that you don't agree with? What are they? Why don't you agree with them? Can you provide any facts or opinions to challenge their thinking?

4. What important ideas haven't been raised in your videoconference yet? Would raising these ideas add to the current conversation, or would they end up interrupting the good thinking that is already happening?

After Your Conference

1. How has your thinking about the topic we are studying in class changed now that you have had the chance to speak to your digital guests? Are there any new ideas you are dying to explore? Do you doubt any ideas that you once believed were true?

2. What caught you off guard or left you wondering during your conversation with your digital guests—either about the topic we have been studying or the people you were speaking to?

3. How would you explain any of the similarities between your thinking and the thinking of your digital guests? Why would they think the same way that you do about the topic we have been studying?

4. How would you explain any of the differences between your thinking and the thinking of your digital guests? What is it about their circumstances or experiences that led them to draw different conclusions about our topic of study than you?

5. Who would you like to speak to next about the topic we have been studying? Why would this be an interesting person or group to speak to? What questions would you try to answer in that conversation?

CHAPTER FIVE

Exploring Collaborative Problem Solving

For the students involved in Michael Furdyk's DeforestACTION initiative (http://dfa.tigweb .org)—an extension of Microsoft's Asia Pacific Partners in Learning Program designed to empower learners to "take control of the planet that they will inherit" by fighting back against global deforestation—learning is anything but traditional. Instead of working on isolated lessons with small handfuls of individual classmates, participants are mastering required curricular objectives while simultaneously wrestling with a complex real-world problem—a practice that educational expert Michael Fullan (2013) describes as an example of meaningful pedagogy in action:

> Over 80,000 students from more than 60 countries are developing as global citizens by collaborating to solve global problems; reviewing and evaluating the causes, impact and politics of deforestation at the local and global levels; analyzing, planning, and organizing by using collaborative technology; preparing and implementing action plans by engaging in interactive activities; and taking part in valuable conversations with peers and mentors. (p. 50)

For Fullan, collaborative problem-solving projects centered on real-world issues like deforestation matter because they create the kinds of engaged learning spaces that students crave. Motivation for learning moves from earning grades to doing meaningful work with others when students study global challenges together. Projects like DeforestACTION are also important, Fullan argues, because they help develop students who are ready to take an action orientation to the world around them. "We believe that if we are going to invest money, time and other resources in purchasing and integrating technology it needs to be hugely value added with respect to student learning," he writes. "Moreover, it needs to lead to the development of 21st Century skills and ways of thinking required by students to be global critical citizens who can help change the world for the better" (Fullan, 2013, p. 53).

How often do these kinds of real-world, problem-centered learning experiences happen in your classrooms? If you work in traditional brick-and-mortar schools, your answer is likely to be discouraging. Current models of standards-based instruction don't always lend themselves to a problem-based approach to learning, which can be time consuming and messy. Many creative teachers, however, have been designing instruction this way for years with amazing success. While it is not enough to simply design problems and turn students loose—mastery depends on teachers who can help students understand the content connected to the initial challenge, the steps necessary to solve problems, and the skills necessary to collaborate—it is possible to make your classroom a place in which creativity and innovation around meaningful questions play central roles in mastering the required curriculum.

This chapter begins with a review of what research says about the three levels of problems. Then, we examine the important role that collaboration can play in developing collectively intelligent solutions to complex problems. Finally, we explore how businesses are using wikis to pair employees in collaborative problem-solving efforts and present a set of tips and tricks for structuring classroom wiki projects. The chapter ends with a series of handouts that can be used to teach students to tackle defined problems without clear solutions and to introduce wikis as a tool for knowledge creation.

In a World Full of Problems

The American philosopher and educational reformer John Dewey (1910) describes the process of problem solving in five logical steps: (1) a difficulty is felt, (2) the difficulty is located and defined, (3) possible solutions are considered, (4) consequences of these solutions are weighed, and (5) one of the solutions is accepted, tested, and evaluated. While students may not work through each step individually or sequentially—especially if they join a team working on a predetermined problem—there is a logical flow involved in developing the most effective solutions to complex problems.

Jacob Getzels, a professor of education at the University of Chicago and noted expert on creativity and problem solving, worked with Mihaly Csikszentmihalyi to take Dewey's thinking one step further, identifying three distinct types of problems (Getzels & Csikszentmihalyi, 1967, 1976).

- **Type 1 problems:** This type of problem is generally the easiest to solve. The problem is clear to both the presenter and the solver, and both are aware of one method for generating the right solution. Type 1 problems involve little more than working systematically to apply a predefined process to discover one "correct answer." Simple mathematics problems—2 + 2, 5 × 4—are examples of Type 1 problems.

- **Type 2 problems:** These problems are also clearly defined for both the presenter and the solver, and while a straightforward method for generating one correct answer exists, neither the method nor the answer are immediately apparent to the solver. Solving Type 2 problems depends first on identifying the right process and then applying that process to generate a solution. Mathematics word problems—If Johnny has eight slices of pizza and he sells each for two dollars, how much money will he raise?—are straightforward examples of Type 2 problems.

- **Type 3 problems:** The problem, the method for working toward resolution, and the complete range of potential outcomes are ambiguous and poorly defined to both the presenter and the solver in Type 3 problems. Solving Type 3 problems begins by defining the exact nature of the challenge: What is being asked? Are there solutions for this problem? Is this a problem worth solving? Then, solvers identify and evaluate potential solutions, selecting the one most likely to resolve the original challenge.

Unlike Type 1 and 2 problems, Type 3 problems have no clear correct answers. In fact, presenters and solvers often interpret the problem and develop solutions differently based on their background of experiences. The problem that students in Michael Furdyk's DeforestACTION project study together—whether we should be concerned by the destruction of the world's forests—is a good example of a Type 3 problem.

Solving challenging problems is a higher-order task requiring students to marshal intellectual resources and develop cognitive strategies. Complex problems must be broken down into manageable chunks. Background experiences—particularly those connected to similar problems—must be consulted. New information must be collected, plans of action must be crafted, and potential solutions must be tested and evaluated. The best problem solvers are persistent, unwilling to surrender, and unafraid of failure. They also possess a measure of confidence in their own abilities, providing the assurance necessary to move forward in the face of ambiguity (Foshay & Kirkley, 2003).

To complicate matters for classroom teachers, simply teaching students specific processes for tackling complex challenges does little to develop problem-solving skills. While working systematically lends important structure to student attempts at problem solving, contextual knowledge is far more important. As Rob Foshay and Jamie Kirkley (2003) write:

> In fact, researchers concluded that knowledge of context was the most critical feature of skill in problem solving. Thus, current research supports problem solving as a situational and context-bound process that depends on the deep structures of knowledge and experience (Palumbo, 1990). When teaching problem solving, authentic problems in realistic contexts are essential. (p. 7)

Solving Type 3 problems effectively—including the kinds of complex, cross-border challenges that Michael Fullan believes should stand at the center of classroom instruction—depends on building problem-specific content knowledge. Solvers who have carefully explored the reasons a problem exists, the impacts of the problem, the emotions evoked by the problem, and the solutions that have already been applied are more likely to develop new and innovative approaches with potential.

Problem-Specific Content Knowledge

Effectively solving Type 3 problems is also a task best left to collaborative groups. In fact, as James Surowiecki (2004) argues in *The Wisdom of Crowds*, individual expertise is almost impossible to develop in areas as broad and intangible as problem solving. "Auto repair, piloting, skiing, perhaps even management: these are skills that yield to application, hard work, and native talent," writes

Surowiecki (2004). "But forecasting an uncertain future and deciding the best course of action in the face of that future are much less likely to do so" (Kindle location 648–653). Individual experts working to solve complex problems are consistently outperformed by groups, draw conclusions contradictory to those held by other experts in the same field, and overestimate the reliability of their own conclusions (Surowiecki, 2004).

In a culture that has a long history of venerating experts, this conclusion can be hard to swallow. Simple proof, though, can be found in one of the most unlikely places: *Who Wants to be a Millionaire*, the once-popular game show hosted by Regis Philbin that pits ordinary Americans against a series of fifteen increasingly complex questions. Answer all fifteen questions correctly, the show promised contestants, and walk away a millionaire; stumble, however, and walk away with nothing. The show's real attention-grabber was pairing each contestant with three unique lifelines. When stumped by difficult questions, the contestant could delete two multiple-choice options, call a friend for consultation, or conduct an instant survey of the studio audience.

For the average viewer watching from home, lifelines—particularly phoning a friend and polling the audience—were the highlight of every episode. And with thousands of dollars at stake, advice drawn from individual expertise or the collective intelligence of a randomly assembled crowd of people could either change a contestant's life or leave him or her empty-handed. With the benefit of hindsight, most contestants would have turned to the random crowd instead of their handpicked experts every time: over the course of the show's history, studio audiences picked the right answer 91 percent of the time (Surowiecki, 2004).

Nothing in Surowiecki's study of the wisdom of crowds—including the results of popular game shows—suggests that individual expertise doesn't exist. As Surowiecki (2004) explains,

> It does mean that however well-informed and sophisticated an expert is, his advice and predictions should be pooled with others to get the most out of him . . . the group's decision will consistently be better decision after decision, while the performance of human experts will vary dramatically depending on the problem they are asked to solve. (Kindle location 681–690)

According to Surowiecki, groups must be cognitively diverse, independent, and decentralized in order to solve complex problems effectively. Groups that are cognitively diverse—easily created in classrooms—include individuals with a range of aptitudes, ideas, and personal interests. When groups are cognitively diverse, they are more likely to consider a range of potential solutions to shared problems simply because members draw from unique sets of background experiences. In every field dependent on innovation, most of the early solutions proposed in group projects will fail or be abandoned, but having access to multiple perspectives increases the likelihood that the best solutions will be uncovered and polished (Surowiecki, 2004).

The members of collectively intelligent groups also exhibit a high degree of independence from one another. In the context of conversations around group dynamics, independence refers to the ability of members to act as individuals free from the influence of their peers. While team members in any group situation will work to shape the thinking of their peers, the strongest groups see diverse thoughts as sources for potential solutions (Surowiecki, 2004). Independent thinking can be difficult for elementary, middle, and high school students, however, who would rather protect relationships than push contrary positions. As a result, teachers must consistently celebrate groups that embrace independence.

Surowiecki's final condition for group intelligence is a certain level of decentralization. Decentralization—the flexibility to make autonomous decisions and set independent directions—encourages motivation and promotes innovation. Decentralized groups are highly invested in their work, resulting in final products that are carefully polished (Surowiecki, 2004). The challenge for elementary, middle, and high school teachers is that classroom groups often benefit from a certain amount of structure early in their development. Without any guidance, support, or coordination—characteristics of completely decentralized projects—students are likely to become frustrated and work without a clear direction. Too much guidance, support, and coordination, however, stifles the natural creativity necessary to generate novel solutions for knotty problems.

The first step, then, for teachers interested in giving students opportunities to collectively develop solutions for complex real-world problems is to ensure that all groups, whether they are self-selected or teacher assigned, are cognitively diverse. Next, teachers must emphasize the important role that independent thought plays in developing effective solutions. Students must feel comfortable voicing disagreement within groups, a skill introduced in chapter 4; otherwise, ideas with potential are likely to be stifled.

Finally, teachers must delicately balance the benefits of decentralization with the need for structure. Several handouts provided at the end of this chapter can help with this task. The first—"Understanding the Problem" (page 145)—is designed to lead students through a meticulous study of any issue. The second—"Evaluating Potential Solutions" (page 147)—forces students to think carefully about the strengths and weaknesses of their preferred solution for any challenge. Both can help groups develop the problem-specific content knowledge that good solutions depend on.

The final two handouts—"Rating Potential Solutions" (page 149) and "Rating Problem-Solution Pieces" (page 151)—are designed to encourage independence in groups, providing students with a safe way to express disagreement with their peers while working together to imagine new solutions for complex problems.

Wikis as a Tool for Collaborative Problem Solving

For businesses in increasingly competitive marketplaces, every day brings new Type 3 problems to solve: Which products are the most likely to catch fire in the next six months? How can we convince consumers to invest in our products even as disposable income becomes a smaller line item in personal budgets? What services can we offer to improve the shopping experience in our stores? Where can we save money? Businesses, therefore, are perfect case studies for teachers interested in learning more about collaborative problem solving in action.

In many companies, these types of questions are answered by small handfuls of executives working at the top of complex hierarchies. Senior management teams establish vision, make important decisions, and give directions. While channels for communication make it theoretically possible for entry-level employees to suggest improvements that can impact the entire organization, the process is poorly defined and slow. Expertise, rather than collective intelligence, drives corporate problem solving in these organizations (Tapscott & Williams, 2006).

The consumer electronics giant Best Buy, however, realized early on that important insight rested in the hearts and minds of its employees—including those working on the sales floors in their two thousand stores. Even with detailed statistical reports tracking every purchase made from the multibillion dollar corporation, senior executives working from the company headquarters in Richfield, Minnesota, understood that they couldn't possibly tell store managers or associates in rural Kansas or the Atlanta suburbs which products and services their customers would be drawn to. They lacked a nuanced understanding of local context—and in an industry competing over the smallest margins, local context could mean the difference between success and failure. Recognizing this, Best Buy set out to tap into the wisdom of its very own crowd—155,000 employees spread out over fifty states and five countries (Tapscott & Williams, 2006).

Under the leadership of Robert Stephens, the thirty-seven-year-old founder of Best Buy's innovative Geek Squad tech services team, the company rolled out an entire collection of collaborative tools bundled in a private digital network called Blue Shirt Nation designed to systematically capture and organize the shared knowledge of their organization. Particularly important to these efforts was a corporate wiki on which employees created an unbelievable amount of shared content. Projects were managed, products were developed, and troubleshooting guides were posted and polished by fifteen thousand voluntary contributors. Sales associates finally had access to the tips and tricks of their peers, and senior managers finally had access to the minds of their most invested employees—a cognitively diverse, independent, and decentralized group (Tapscott & Williams, 2006).

The question most often asked by those considering wikis as a tool for developing meaningful solutions to shared problems is, Why do people participate? After all, the thousands of volunteers actively creating content in Blue Shirt Nation are not being rewarded in the traditional sense for their contributions. According to Jimmy Wales—the founder of Wikipedia, the world's most notable wiki—three factors motivate people to voluntarily coproduce content.

1. **Opportunities to interact with other people:** As we learned in chapter 4, humans are naturally driven to connect. While the connections between individuals coproducing content on Wikipedia and Blue Shirt Nation are primarily digital, any opportunity to work together on a shared task can be engaging. "Why do people play softball?" asks Wales. "It is fun, it is a social activity" (as cited in Tapscott & Williams, 2006, Kindle location 1315–1322).

2. **Opportunities to interact with motivating content:** The Best Buy Geek Squad takes real pride in their role as technology savants. While they are unlikely to spend any time documenting the seasons of the past ten Super Bowl Champions, turn them loose to design a

better jump drive—an actual task that Best Buy asked of the Geek Squad—and you will get hundreds of polished sketches and interesting designs. Collaborative problem solving, then, depends on content that motivates participants.

3. **Opportunities to work toward a meaningful shared outcome:** Jimmy Wales isn't surprised that millions of pages of content have been created on Wikipedia by volunteers. "We are gathering together to build this resource that will be made available to all of the people of the world," argues Wales. "That's a goal that people can get behind" (as cited in Tapscott & Williams, 2006, Kindle location 1322–1328). Voluntary coproduction projects are more likely to be successful when they share a significant and meaningful outcome (Tapscott & Williams, 2006).

What lessons can teachers learn from Wikipedia and Best Buy about the role that wikis can play as tools in classrooms? Perhaps most importantly, the characteristics of successful corporate wiki efforts mirror the characteristics of the kinds of problem-centered learning experiences described at the beginning of this chapter. In classrooms that are moving learning forward, students "talk of doing things that are meaningful in the world, projects that focus on solving a problem, engaging in teamwork, and operating under conditions that encourage risk-taking" (Fullan, 2013, p. 23). Those characteristics shouldn't come as a surprise to most teachers. Our best lessons have always included opportunities for students to interact with one another around motivating content and to work toward meaningful shared outcomes. Because wikis *enable* those core behaviors, they should be a natural fit for supporting collaborative problem-solving projects in classrooms.

Classroom Wiki Projects

Perhaps the reason Wikipedia and Blue Shirt Nation are so appealing and powerful is that users independently self-select the kinds of contributions they want to make. Most begin by following updates on topics that fuel their personal interests. They check new content for accuracy, correct mistakes, and polish the format of existing entries. They insert links and challenge users who post inaccurate information. They serve as de facto custodians, policing the content they care about—sometimes working alone and other times developing partnerships with digital peers who share the same passions (Tapscott & Williams, 2006).

Other users adopt specific roles across categories by inserting links, translating content, adding images, and checking citations. Because these roles are self-defined, there is a high level of intrinsic motivation. No one is telling Wikipedia or Blue Shirt Nation users that they have to contribute, and yet the collective effort of a diverse group of users inevitably results in interesting final products containing extensive content (Tapscott & Williams, 2006).

While this uniquely organic model for the peer production of content works well for Wikipedia and Blue Shirt Nation, it can be a recipe for disaster in elementary, middle, and high school classrooms simply because teachers and students are often initially unsure of exactly what good wiki work looks like. Understanding the characteristics of successful projects, then, is a critical first step toward structuring any collaborative wiki efforts in your classroom. Those characteristics—introduced to students in the "Characteristics of Quality Wiki Pages" worksheet (page 152)—include accurate content, deep linking, evidence of group revision, and quality presentation.

Accurate Content

The initial fear that every teacher has when approaching work with wikis is the constant risk that students will learn to embrace a tool that may promote the sharing of inaccurate content or flawed ideas. Because wikis are open websites that can be edited by anyone, the content on wikis is often changing. At any given time, wikis can contain information that is just plain wrong.

That same risk, however, can make wikis a valuable teaching tool! The most accomplished wiki educators don't shy away from inaccurate content posted on classroom wiki projects. Instead, they embrace it as an opportunity to teach students about the importance of judging the reliability of online sources. While they constantly push students to proofread for precision, they also recognize that content errors are new opportunities to teach students about information literacy.

Deep Linking

Higher-level learning experiences require learners to read and react to information. Synthesizing and evaluating content created by others is essential before new understandings can be developed. In wiki work, evidence of synthesis and evaluation can be seen in the number and quality of resources linked to on a wiki page. As authors develop new content, they insert links from a variety of reliable sources to provide evidence supporting their thinking.

Deep linking in classroom wiki projects forces students to make connections between their own beliefs and external evidence. It also serves as an additional opportunity for classrooms to have conversations about judging the reliability of online sources. Wiki pages with extensive links to credible sources are more likely to be trustworthy than those with limited links to questionable sources.

Evidence of Group Revision

Wikis are designed for collaboration, plain and simple. They are tools that facilitate the asynchronous work of peers around content of shared interest. As a result, accomplished academic wiki pages have evidence of extensive group revision. Page discussion boards include ongoing conversations about quality and content, and a careful exploration of the page history button (generally found somewhere in the header or footer of each wiki page) will reveal an extensive collection of previous versions.

In many ways, group revision is the greatest challenge for teachers interested in incorporating wiki work into their classrooms because students are inherently tentative about making meaningful edits to one another's work. Used in largely isolated classrooms where collaboration has generally been somewhat simple or superficial, peers use wiki pages as places to post their own content rather than to make changes to content posted by others. Over time and with constant modeling, however, students embrace the collective nature of wiki pages and start making meaningful revisions to the work of their peers.

Quality Presentation

Accomplished wikis are really no different from accomplished writing in any other format: they demonstrate the use of age-appropriate grammar, punctuation, and spelling. Writers recognize that effective communication depends on their ability to create pieces that are easy to understand and are unencumbered by mistakes.

For many teachers, wikis become natural forums for reviewing grammar and spelling rules with students. Because errors are almost always going to be present in constantly changing work being created by kids, wikis offer real-world opportunities for proofreading practice. Accomplished wikis also demonstrate age-appropriate levels of visual presentation. Images and embedded video are often used to enhance wiki pages. Creators maintain a balance, however, between appropriate use of multimedia content and digital overkill, recognizing that interactive elements can distract readers.

Wiki Roles

Look carefully at the revision history of any Wikipedia entry, and you will notice that the majority of the work is done by a small handful of people—over 50 percent of Wikipedia's edits are made by less than 1 percent of its users (Tapscott & Williams, 2006). In school-based wiki efforts, this level of unbalanced participation can be detrimental—especially when students are working on graded group projects designed to demonstrate mastery of required learning outcomes. In these situations, it is essential for teachers to introduce a set of defined roles for student participation. Not only can defined roles balance participation, but they can also serve as an introduction to the kinds of shared tasks that Wikipedians—who model successful collaborative efforts to create knowledge-based content every day—complete naturally.

The following roles can serve as a good starting point for your classroom's collaborative problem-solving projects: Link Layer, Flow Master, Spelling Cop, Discussion Starter, and Captain Spit-and-Polish.

Link Layer

As we described earlier, links are essential in wiki projects, because they allow authors to synthesize content and allow readers to explore on their own. The credibility of an entire site, therefore, depends on the quality of the links included. What's more, links help teachers quickly assess levels of understanding and common misconceptions about topics by comparing the assertions being made on a group's wiki page to the content included in their collection of links.

Successful student projects, then, depend on the Link Layer, who is responsible for reviewing every link included on their group's wiki pages. Link Layers should begin by identifying logical places to insert links in their group's work, find sources that align nicely with the conclusions of their collaborative partners, and check each site selected for bias or accuracy. Finally, Link Layers must be willing to replace any links to questionable websites that have been included in their group's work.

Flow Master

Often, the greatest challenge for students when collaborating on wikis is naturally blending the language styles and organizing strategies of multiple authors. Trained to work on a single piece from beginning to end, students rarely consider how well their contributions will work with the content already added by peers. The consequences: poorly structured pieces that are difficult to read and understand.

That's where Flow Masters come in. Flow Masters read a group's wiki page with a critical eye, looking for places where readers are likely to be confused. They polish language, ensure a unified voice throughout the piece, and check to be sure that content is organized logically. The challenge for Flow Masters is that wiki pages are constantly changing, which means that Flow Masters must constantly revise. Flow Masters make the kinds of revisions that improve the readability of their group's final product.

Spelling Cop

Surrounded by informal opportunities to communicate that are driven by speed and aimed at peers—text messages, Facebook updates, instant messages—iGeners rarely place a priority on precise language. The results include poor writing habits that lead to final products riddled with simple spelling errors regardless of their intended audience.

Collaborative wikis focused on important issues provide teachers with the perfect opportunity to stress the central role that accuracy plays in building credibility and earning the confidence of readers. Accuracy, however, depends on having a meticulous Spelling Cop in each group who is responsible for checking every word added to a shared final product. While the Spelling Cop's role appears simple, it requires persistence. Each new revision is an opportunity for another word to be misspelled!

Discussion Starter

Like most of the work spotlighted in *Teaching the iGeneration*, good wiki projects rely on conversations between students. The difference is that the conversations between partners in wiki projects are almost always focused on the steps necessary for efficient and effective peer production. Coordination is essential in any shared effort, and Discussion Starters are largely responsible for starting the kinds of conversations that can organize their group.

Discussion Starters live on the discussion boards of shared wiki pages. They are responsible for asking questions about what their group is producing. They must be good evaluators, comparing their group's product and progress against the work being done by others. They must also be good planners, helping their group set due dates and complete required tasks, and good motivators, capable of providing encouragement and direction whenever necessary.

Captain Spit-and-Polish

In chapter 3, we learned that visual influence is becoming increasingly important in our world. Capturing the attention of iGeners—who have lived their entire lives connected to televisions, video games, and the Internet—depends on the careful use of graphics, images, colors, and font sizes. What's more, interactive content is remembered while static content is quickly forgotten.

Captain Spit-and-Polish is responsible for incorporating content that is visually appealing and capable of capturing the attention of viewers likely to scan first and read later. They use images, videos and other embeddable content to support arguments and assertions. They also work to ensure that the layout of their wiki page is professional and interesting. The trickiest part of Captain Spit-and-Polish's job is remembering who the intended audience for a particular page is and making sure that all graphics, images, and layout decisions are appropriate for that unique group of people. The kinds of content that appeal to twelve-year-olds probably won't appeal to anyone over twenty-two!

Implementation Strategies for Wiki Beginners

Once your students are comfortable with the characteristics of good wiki work and are aware of a set of specific, defined roles for participation, you will be ready to start projects using wikis as a tool for the coproduction of content around complex problems. To make this work more approachable and productive, consider the following suggestions: start with one classroom wiki, model classroom wiki projects around Wikipedia pages, provide groups with initial structures to follow and content to explore, use wikis to enrich and remediate, keep wikis open for viewing but closed for revision, and name and train student editors.

Start With One Classroom Wiki

At their core, wikis are about sharing information. Students working together can use wikis to generate a documented collection of shared solutions to complex global problems built from the collective intelligence of a group. The challenge, however, is finding enough content to fill a wiki. That's why it is best to keep your initial efforts simple and clean by creating wiki projects completed by entire classes instead of individual students. Consider having small groups design, monitor, and manage stand-alone pages in shared classroom wikis rather than creating and maintaining entire wikis on their own. Doing so will ensure that your wiki builds quickly without overwhelming anyone.

Model Classroom Wiki Projects Around Wikipedia Pages

Whether traditional teachers like it or not, Wikipedia will likely remain the most visible example of wikis in action for a long, long while. It has caught the attention of millions of users already, is built on simple and sustainable software, and taps into the natural human desire to share. Because of its size and influence—and because your students are likely to have used Wikipedia as a research source at some point in their school careers—consider using Wikipedia as a model for your own classroom wiki projects. Conceptually, using Wikipedia as a model for your classroom wiki project will make your expectations approachable—and give students samples to refer to while completing their final products.

Provide Groups With Initial Structures to Follow and Content to Explore

While using Wikipedia as a conceptual model may provide your students with a sense of what you are trying to create, it may also completely backfire. Wikipedia is, after all, a vast resource with sophisticated and polished entries on an almost mind-boggling number of topics. Your students may end up absolutely intimidated when looking at your blank wiki on the first day of your classroom project and knowing that Wikipedia is the standard to be compared against!

To make initial efforts seem more doable, work to add extensive content to your classroom wiki ahead of time. Create page templates complete with tables of contents that detail required information—description of problem, potential solutions, fatal flaws, final thoughts—for each group. Design one or two sample pages that students can refer to. Including extensive collections of supporting materials that students can use while researching will help them get started. Another way to jumpstart the process is to share simple step-by-step directions for using the wiki tool that you have selected, post checklists and rubrics that can guide student work, and point to sources of embeddable content—photo warehouses, video sharing sites, free digital tools for creating interactive content—that students may find useful. Systematically frontloading your classroom wiki can help convince your classes that they *can* produce an impressive final product rivaling Wikipedia.

Use Wikis to Enrich and Remediate

For many classroom teachers, finding differentiated learning opportunities can be an intimidating task. Classroom wikis, however—especially those designed to detail solutions to problems connected to required classroom content—can make independent work simple for everyone.

Advanced students can create new pages for your wiki and introduce challenging concepts in approachable ways. Students who finish work early can proofread content for accuracy, correct factual errors, add essential information, and point out flaws in the solutions proposed by their peers. Using classroom wikis as tools for differentiation will help make the time and energy that you invest in organizing wiki work worthwhile—and will help your students see your wiki as a valuable learning tool instead of simply as a graded task to be forgotten.

Keep Wikis Open for Viewing but Closed for Revision

All wiki services provide users with a wide range of viewing and editing settings. Wikis can be completely closed, requiring users to log in to see and edit content, or completely open, allowing anyone to view and edit without invitation. The best starting point for classroom wiki projects is to leave your wiki open for viewing but to extend editing privileges to just the students in your classroom.

By doing so, you will not only ensure that your students benefit from the motivation of creating work that can be seen by a larger audience, but also that the content created by your classes can't be destroyed by outsiders simply looking to cause trouble. Extending editing privileges to just the students in your classroom also means that you will be able to monitor the kinds of work that each student is doing online. If you choose to grade contributions to classroom wiki projects, you can quickly identify the changes made under each student's username and hold students accountable for their digital contributions.

Name and Train Student Editors

Teachers may find that monitoring ongoing wiki projects for quality can be overwhelming, especially when students are highly motivated and making dozens of revisions per day. Uncomfortable with unmonitored pages and unable to find the time to keep up with the new work being added to classroom wikis, teachers end up pulling the plug on projects rather than risk being embarrassed by poor final products. To avoid this all-too-common end result, train student editors, as mentioned in chapter 2, to be responsible for tracking the changes made to individual pages in your classroom project.

Student editors can visit wiki pages several times a week, checking new contributions for accuracy and appearance. When errors are found, student editors can make instant changes or contact student authors and ask that they polish the work they have added. Page monitoring responsibilities can be assigned based on a student's demonstrated interest in a topic of study, motivation to revise and edit content, or willingness to take responsibility for a classroom's collective efforts.

The list of tasks that students must complete to create quality wiki pages (page 154), the checklist outlining the steps that teachers must take to successfully implement classroom wiki work (page 156), and the scoring rubric that can be used to evaluate wiki products (page 159) found at the end of this chapter can help you reinforce these suggestions while working with classroom wiki projects.

Final Thoughts

Rich Lehrer—a teacher at the Brookwood School in Manchester, Massachusetts, and a regular participant in the Challenge 20/20 projects organized by the National Association of Independent Schools (2014)—has spent the past few years exploring the role that biomass cook stoves can play in replacing charcoal ovens in primitive kitchens with the students in his eighth-grade science classes. While that topic may seem surprising at first—the kids in Lehrer's classes aren't likely to be forced to cook anything over an open fire in a primitive kitchen in order to provide dinner for their families—the work has left his students inspired. Their goal: to help students in their partner class in Brazil, a developing country where breathing in the smoke of kitchen fires leads to two million deaths from respiratory illness a year, to live better lives (Cutler, 2013).

Lehrer's efforts are a model of the kinds of collaborative problem-solving projects that Paul Miller—director of Global Initiatives for the National Association of Independent Schools—believes in. "There are critical problems that are facing the entire world, and the thinking is that it's not sufficient to wait for students to graduate, get jobs, and reach a point where they might have sufficient authority to address any of the these issues," he argues. "What we really need is for them to start addressing these issues right away . . . One of the ways that allows them to work their way to that point is the Challenge 20/20 Program" (as cited in Cutler, 2013).

Lehrer's efforts are also a glimpse into the future of how problem solving will be taught. Motivated to make connections and not limited by physical boundaries, students will be using new media tools—video games, wikis, discussion boards, videoconferencing applications—to collaborate on complex, real-world problems together. In the process, they will study motivating content, explore new careers, and reflect on foreign situations. More importantly, they will begin to look inside the minds of peers from all over the world, understanding that global challenges are seen through different lenses and recognizing that solutions cannot be nation-specific. Finally, they will learn to see colleagues from other countries as allies whose intelligence and ability is only a mouse-click away.

Will your students be ready to solve problems collaboratively in an increasingly connected world that faces a broad range of seemingly insurmountable, borderless challenges?

Curriculum Matters: The Next Generation Science Standards

The engineering strands of the Next Generation Science Standards expect students to be able to "define problems more precisely" and "to conduct a more thorough process of choosing the best solution" (NGSS Lead States, 2013). This means that students must learn to reflect deeply about problems, create criteria for evaluating potential solutions that include a careful consideration of impacts on society and the environment, and combine disparate ideas into a new solution "that may be better than any of the preliminary ideas" (NGSS Lead States, 2013).

Do these skills also appear in the curricula for your classes? Are they skills that you believe are important for iGeners? Which activities, strategies, and tools presented in this chapter would help students master these skills?

Understanding the Problem

The first challenge that any concerned citizen must face when tackling global challenges is to understand a problem as completely as possible before evaluating solutions. Understanding a problem begins by studying statistics, opinions, emotions, and impacts. Use this handout to shape your understanding of the global challenge we are studying in class. Remember to evaluate the sources you are studying for reliability and bias and to use http://bitly.com to shorten web addresses.

Type of Evidence	Evidence	Sources
Statistics are often the most convincing bit of evidence you can find when evaluating global challenges. By finding numbers that describe your problem today, over time, or in the future, you will get a better sense of just how big the issue you are dealing with is.		
In an increasingly connected world in which people can publish their thoughts easily, there are going to be *tons* of different people expressing *tons* of different **opinions** about any global challenge that you choose to study. Some will try to explain the source of the issue or challenge your studying. Others will detail potential consequences if your global challenge goes unaddressed. Reading through these opinions will turn you on to potential starting points for your solution planning.		
While statistics can be convincing and opinions can serve as starting points for your solution planning, **emotions** will always influence how important your problem really is and should always influence the choices you make when crafting solutions. After all, solutions are useless if they are wildly unpopular! As you work through your research, pay attention to passions. What do people feel strongly about? Why? Are passions different depending on locations? How might this change your solution planning?		

Type of Evidence	Evidence	Sources
In the end, the global challenge you are studying has an **impact** on our planet in some significant way—otherwise it wouldn't be a global issue at all! While it is likely that you will be able to find evidence of the impact that your global challenge is having on the world in the statistics, opinions, and emotions that you are collecting, it is important to create a clear, prioritized list of impacts before designing solutions. Otherwise, your work will be unfocused and careless.		

Summarizing Statement: After collecting statistics, opinions, emotions, and impacts related to the global challenge you are studying, write a paragraph summarizing important points to remember about your problem. Check with your group mates to see if you have left anything important out of your summary. Resolve any group disagreements by coming to consensus about what is most important to consider when developing potential solutions.

Evaluating Potential Solutions

Finding solutions for global challenges is a complex task that requires careful thinking. Use the following checklist to evaluate the quality of the solutions that your group is considering. Remember that the best research projects will review several potential solutions.

Name of Potential Solution:

1. How will your solution fix the problem we are studying in class? Can it be implemented everywhere, or will it only be effective for some people living in some places?

2. What is unique about your potential solution? Is it an idea that will catch the attention of leaders? Of businesses? Of individuals?

3. How difficult will it be to implement your solution? Are there obvious barriers that will cause your solution to fail, or is it likely that your solution will be an instant success? Why?

4. What kinds of costs will your solution carry? Will your suggestions be too expensive? Will your solution take too long to implement to be worthwhile?

5. Will your solution create any new problems? What are they likely to be? Are those new problems serious enough to make your solution essentially useless?

6. What kinds of groups will naturally oppose your solution? Why? Are there legitimate reasons for their resistance? How will you address those concerns in your final proposal?

7. Are there any alternatives to the solution you are studying? What are they? Would these alternatives be easier to implement? Would they carry fewer costs? Have fewer opponents?

8. Has your solution ever been implemented before? Where? What were the results? Do you have links to evidence of outcomes that you can share in your research project?

Rating Potential Solutions

While working with your partners to select the best solutions for the global challenge we are studying in class, you will need a way to come to consensus with one another. Use the following rating scale to start conversations about each of the potential solutions you are considering.

Rating: 5

- This is a solution I believe in.
- This solution will be easy to implement, and its costs won't scare people away.
- This solution has no natural opponents or likely enemies. It is an idea that everyone can support.
- This is a solution that I know can succeed—either because it has already been implemented successfully or because the potential barriers to the solution are simple to overcome.
- I'm ready to recommend this solution to anyone, and I know it is going to work!

Rating: 4

- This solution has a ton of potential.
- The barriers to implementing this solution seem relatively simple to overcome, and there are no natural opponents or likely enemies to our idea.
- The costs for this solution are not extraordinary.
- The only thing that causes me to hesitate is that this solution has never been implemented successfully before—which means that there are no guarantees that our idea will work!
- I've got enough confidence in this solution to recommend it, however. Let's get started.

Rating: 3

- This solution hasn't convinced me yet.
- While there are some real strengths to pursuing this idea, there are also some real risks that I'm not sure can be resolved easily.
- We might be recommending an idea that is impossible to pull off because of the costs attached or because the barriers to success are too high.
- We might also be recommending an idea that people won't support.
- I'll need more evidence before I'm willing to recommend this solution to others.

Rating: 2

- Sitting here right now, I couldn't recommend this solution to others. There are too many risks and too few rewards.
- This solution might be too costly to really pull off. What's more, there are probably going to be a bunch of people opposed to this solution.
- I don't think this solution will be ready in time to solve the problem we are trying to address.
- I've got serious doubts about this solution. I'll move forward, but only with caution and only after doing a lot more research.

page 1 of 2

Teaching the iGeneration © 2015 Solution Tree Press • solution-tree.com
Visit **go.solution-tree.com/technology** or **plugusin.pbworks.com** to download this page.

Rating: 1
▪ This solution seems like a bad idea.
▪ Our idea has never been tried before by anyone.
▪ What's more, there are obvious barriers that we are going to have to overcome if our solution is going to succeed—and I don't think it is possible to overcome those barriers.
▪ To work, someone is going to have to invest tons of time, energy, and money into our solution, and time, energy, and money are always hard to come by.
▪ What's worse is that I'm pretty sure our solution will create a whole new set of problems!
▪ I don't think I'm willing to move forward with this solution.

Rating: 0
▪ This solution will never work.
▪ There is plenty of evidence to prove that this solution is too expensive or impractical to even work.
▪ There are open enemies who we will need to convince before we will even come close to getting others to believe in our solution—and even then, I'm pretty sure that this solution will fail.
▪ There is no sense in even considering this solution.

Rating Problem-Solution Pieces

Let's face it, not all problem-solution pieces are created equally! Some are more likely to convince readers to take action than others. Use this handout to rate the overall quality of the problem-solution pieces that you review.

Your Work Is Amazing

- Your problem-solution piece is amazing.
- As I was reading your work, I was completely convinced that there was a real problem that needed to be solved.
- You included all kinds of evidence—both about the problem and the potential solutions—and you seemed to take any controversial emotions and opinions into account.
- Most importantly, though, you made it seem urgent for me to take action and then provided a set of potential solutions that I can start working on tomorrow.

You Got It

- Your problem-solution piece was pretty impressive.
- You did a good job convincing me that there was a real problem that needed to be addressed, and you clearly outlined a set of solutions.
- I'm not totally convinced that the all of your solutions are realistic, though. While they sound good on paper, one or two may prove to be impossible to pull off—either because they are too costly, too impractical, or opposed by too many people.
- All in all, there are far more strengths in your piece than weaknesses.

You Are Getting There

- Your problem-solution piece has left me wondering.
- You mention a problem that I know is real. In fact, I've heard about it enough times that I really want to take action to help.
- You also mention solutions that I'll bet will actually work. They are certainly believable and interesting.
- I'd love to see more evidence—both to persuade me that your problem is urgent and that your solutions will work.

Celebrations and Suggestions

1. What can we celebrate about this particular piece? Has the author tackled an issue that other readers will believe in? Are there interesting solutions that just might work? What are they?

2. What suggestions do you have for improving this piece? Are there solutions that seem questionable? Places where you'd like to see more evidence provided? What next steps would you take if this was your work?

Characteristics of Quality Wiki Pages

One of the first steps to creating a quality wiki page is to spend time exploring other student wiki pages. Working with your research group, use the following handout to evaluate at least one of the wiki pages listed below. Each was designed by groups of sixth-grade students who were presenting potential solutions for global warming. Remember to note what was impressive about the wiki page that you evaluate, any ideas you would like to copy, and what you would improve about the work.

Wiki Samples:

The Solution to Pollution	The Green Squad	The Global Warming Girls
http://bit.ly/1uEbjKw	http://bit.ly/1FBHmTN	http://bit.ly/1wjYdFs

Questions to Consider

1. Does the wiki page have an appealing layout that makes reading and exploring easy? Have subtitles or a table of contents been used to organize the information? Were they needed?

   Your Response / Next Steps:

2. Is the content on this wiki page accurate and engaging? Have the authors included links to reliable external sources that you can explore to verify their information? Are you convinced by the arguments presented by this student group?

   Your Response / Next Steps:

3. Have interesting images and embedded content like videos or slideshows been included to catch the attention of readers? Would readers be drawn in or distracted by this extra content?

   Your Response / Next Steps:

4. Has the content on this wiki page been proofread carefully? Do typing errors or grammar mistakes get in the way of your understanding? Do you have to work to make sense of the content?

    Your Response / Next Steps:

5. Have the authors of this wiki page used the comment section in a meaningful way to plan their work? Is there evidence that this project was a collective effort, or does it look like most of the work was done by one or two group members?

    Your Response / Next Steps:

Wiki Tasks for Student Groups

One of the best ways for your research group to report about the global challenge you are studying in class is to create a wiki page. After your teacher creates student accounts for everyone in your class and introduces you to the basics of wiki work, use the following checklist to organize your group's collective efforts.

Questions to Consider

1. Does every member of your group understand how to add content—text, images, links, video—and make edits to your shared wiki page?

    Your Response / Next Steps:

2. Does your group have a Link Layer, who will insert links to reliable external sources throughout your shared wiki page? Does your Link Layer know the characteristics of websites that can't be trusted?

    Your Response / Next Steps:

3. Does your group have a Flow Master who will edit your text for readability? Is this person an accomplished writer comfortable with making changes?

    Your Response / Next Steps:

4. Does your group have a Spelling Cop who will ensure that there are no spelling errors in your final product?

    Your Response / Next Steps:

Teaching the iGeneration © 2010, 2015 Solution Tree Press • solution-tree.com
Visit **go.solution-tree.com/technology** or **plugusin.pbworks.com** to download this page.

5. Does your group have a Discussion Starter who will start conversations about the progress and quality of your group's work in the comment section of your shared wiki page? Will your Discussion Starter regularly visit the wiki pages being created by other student groups to collect ideas and make comparisons to your work?

    Your Response / Next Steps:

6. Does your group have a Captain Spit-and-Polish who will add images, manage formatting, and embed interesting content to make your shared wiki page more engaging?

    Your Response / Next Steps:

7. Has your group set a starting date and an ending date for adding content and making changes to your shared wiki page that everyone can agree to?

    Your Response / Next Steps:

Teaching the iGeneration © 2010, 2015 Solution Tree Press • solution-tree.com
Visit **go.solution-tree.com/technology** or **plugusin.pbworks.com** to download this page.

Teacher Checklist for Wiki Projects

Like blogs, wikis are one of the most accessible tools available to classroom teachers new to digital projects. Teachers can often quickly and easily translate tasks that their students are already responsible for completing into wiki projects. The following questions will help you determine whether or not you are prepared to facilitate wiki projects in your classroom.

Technical and Procedural Preparations

1. Does your school or district's technology services department have a preferred wiki service?

Your Response / Next Steps:

2. Are you aware of any Internet safety policies or procedures in place at the school or district level that may influence your wiki project? Have you introduced your students to basic Internet safety practices?

Your Response / Next Steps:

3. Have you informed parents that their children will be maintaining an online forum for content creation? Are you planning on asking parents to sign a permission slip before students can participate in your wiki project?

Your Response / Next Steps:

4. Have you looked into whether or not the wiki service you are planning to use allows teachers to create individual user accounts for each of the students in their classes or on their teams?

Your Response / Next Steps:

5. Have you developed a comfort level with the basic steps involved in creating content on your wiki? Can you add new pages? Do you know how to add images and links? Have you figured out how to upload files or to comment on pages? Are you comfortable with embedding content?

    Your Response / Next Steps:

6. Have you created a basic structure for your classroom wiki that includes an opening page introducing the purpose for your project and links to new pages where students will add content? Are you planning on developing at least one sample page to guide student work?

    Your Response / Next Steps:

Pedagogical Preparations

1. Have your students explored wiki pages created by other students? Can they identify the characteristics of quality wiki work? Can they point out common flaws in student assignments?

    Your Response / Next Steps:

2. Are your students prepared to give and receive feedback on written work? Will they be comfortable with peers revising and editing their contributions to shared wiki pages?

    Your Response / Next Steps:

3. Do your students understand that the work done on wikis must be carefully edited and proofread in order to earn credibility with readers?

    Your Response / Next Steps:

Teaching the iGeneration © 2010, 2015 Solution Tree Press • solution-tree.com
Visit **go.solution-tree.com/technology** or **plugusin.pbworks.com** to download this page.

4. Are you planning on assigning roles to students working on shared wiki pages in order to structure their work?

   Your Response / Next Steps:

5. Have you modeled the steps involved in starting new pages, adding links, inserting pictures, and embedding interesting content into the final products posted in the wiki service you have chosen to use with students?

   Your Response / Next Steps:

6. Do your students know how to use the links included in the page history of their wiki project to revert to earlier versions if their shared work is inadvertently—or intentionally—destroyed?

   Your Response / Next Steps:

7. Have you considered training a small cadre of student technology leaders to serve as student editors and page monitors? Do these editors have a clear sense of their responsibilities? Will there be any rewards for filling this role?

   Your Response / Next Steps:

Wiki Scoring Rubric

The following questions can be used by groups to self-assess their own products or by teachers to give final scores as your class begins to craft wiki pages designed to present potential solutions to global challenges.

Questions to Consider

1. Has the group provided enough background knowledge on the global challenge for novice readers to make informed decisions?

2. Is there evidence that the group has considered a wide range of potential solutions for the global challenge before making final recommendations?

3. Has the group addressed the most common criticisms that are likely to be leveled against their chosen solutions?

4. Has the group used statistics, opinions, emotions, and impacts effectively to express their point of view? Are readers likely to be influenced by this wiki page?

5. Has the group included extensive links to reliable outside sites designed to provide readers with evidence for central claims or sources for continued study?

6. Has the group used age-appropriate grammar and mechanics? Has the piece been carefully proofread to ensure that mistakes don't interfere with the reader's understanding?

Teaching the iGeneration © 2010, 2015 Solution Tree Press • solution-tree.com
Visit **go.solution-tree.com/technology** or **plugusin.pbworks.com** to download this page.

7. Has the group included visual elements—pictures, charts, graphs, streaming video clips—to make their wiki page more engaging and their message more convincing?

8. Has the group used titles and subtitles—or embedded tables of contents—to organize their wiki page and to make navigation easy?

9. Is there evidence in the page history or on the discussion board that this wiki was a collective project with significant contributions made by all members?

10. Will readers walk away from this wiki page knowing more about the topic being studied and the potential solutions that can be pursued?

Epilogue

This book has been a journey through the mind of the iGeneration learner and an exploration of the kinds of skills being discussed in classrooms, workrooms, and boardrooms at local, state, national, and international levels. As we spend more time meeting with businesses and watching how the U.S. economy is changing, we understand that the jobs of tomorrow are going to depend on students who can use technology to efficiently create, persuade, collaborate, communicate, innovate, and evaluate in knowledge-driven spaces. Given this scenario, it seems apropos to end *Teaching the iGeneration* by hearing from a young learner with strong beliefs about just how schools should change.

Michael is a ten-year-old fifth grader living in the suburbs. His elementary school is only two years old and regularly posts some of the highest standardized test scores in the county. He is an above-average reader, an accomplished mathematician, and an all-around curious kid who should enjoy school. Unfortunately, even at the age of ten, Michael is already starting to find little value in the learning that takes place in his classroom, and he is beginning to disconnect. In order to understand why he feels this way, it is important to look at the differences in how Michael learns at school and at home.

Learning at School

Michael gets dropped off at school each morning around 8:45, in plenty of time to make it to class before the Pledge of Allegiance begins at 9:05. When he enters the classroom, he has morning work to complete—editing a few sentences or completing a math problem or two. Once or twice each week, Michael has to write in his composition notebook. The rest of the day is chunked into blocks of time for math, reading and language arts, science or social studies, lunch, and specials (physical education, music, art, Spanish, or computers). Each block is full of either teacher-directed lessons or small-group instruction.

Michael's math classes look a lot like the math classes that his parents and grandparents sat through. Textbooks are opened, new problems are introduced, solutions are generated, answers are checked, and homework is assigned. Language arts lessons are worksheet driven as teachers push through county pacing guides designed to prepare students for end-of-grade exams. Sometimes projects are used to teach science and social studies content, but minutes are tight and most of the work assigned is completed at home. Class periods are dedicated to collecting information and taking notes. In short, Michael spends a lot of time in his classroom with very little choice in what or how he learns.

Michael's only experiences with technology in school come when he goes to the computer lab—a special scheduled once every other week. There are three computers wired for high-speed Internet access in his classroom, but they are rarely turned on. An interactive whiteboard sits in the media center, but it can only be used by the media specialist. While Michael lives in a community in which students have tons of digital devices at home, students are not allowed to bring their own technology into the school. Even if they could, however, their efforts would be pointless: their building doesn't have a wireless infrastructure yet.

For Michael's parents, homework time is always a grind. While they are both well-educated supporters of public schools, interested in classroom happenings, and capable of offering Michael help with learning almost any subject, his resistance to even trying to get through the required content can be exhausting. Challenging math questions are met with thrown pencils. Reading worksheets are met with tears. Twenty-minute assignments can take an hour's worth of coaxing and support—not to mention a healthy dose of consequences—to complete.

Michael's experiences with school are analogous to flying on an airplane. As you buckle in for the ride, a highly trained pilot—seen as the only real expert on board—explains the plans for the flight, tells you to sit back and relax, and then does all of the real work. Sure, you have some options—flipping through the wrinkled copy of *SkyMall* magazine sitting in your seat back, catching a quick nap, stealing a section of newspaper—but your choices are limited and completely uninteresting. Worse yet, even though you are less than six inches from a hundred other passengers, you spend your time largely alone and looking straight ahead. While you know that your trip is a necessary evil that you can't avoid, all you really want to do is get home.

Learning at Home

In the evenings, Michael usually makes a beeline for one of his family's game systems. The newest is an Xbox One with Xbox Live that lets him connect to the Internet. He also has a tablet, a laptop, and a smartphone—devices shared with his mom and dad and acquired over several years. When he's not playing with one of his video games, chances are good that he is curled up behind one of his family's four computers, which can all access the Internet wirelessly. Regardless of where he is, Michael is connected to the rest of the world, studying things that interest him, and making choices about what to learn—and his choices are as diverse as his interests.

As a part of the LEGO Network (http://mln.lego.com/en-us/network/status.aspx), Michael and his next-door neighbor have been climbing the rank ladder by designing blueprints and collaborating with other kids in a walled social network built around one of his favorite toys, LEGO bricks. While these kinds of opportunities to interact online seem extraordinary to Michael's grandparents, they are ordinary to him. After all, he has never known a web on which he couldn't contribute, make friends, share resources, and upload information.

Michael's journey on the LEGO Network is surprisingly complex. In order to move up the rank ladder—an objective that Michael is intrinsically motivated to achieve—he has to figure out who to contact, what questions to ask, and how to acquire the resources that he needs to build the blueprints he has designed. All of the learning happening in the LEGO Network is directed by Michael. As he moves up in rank, he gains access to additional challenges and can help other people with his new status. When faced with particularly difficult problems, Michael tries many solutions before giving up and reaching out to his friend across the street or turning to YouTube videos for help completing the task. Unlike the homework headaches that are driving his parents nuts, Michael rarely quits on the LEGO Network or asks his mom and dad to do the work for him. He is proud of his level five ranking because he knows he has earned it himself.

When Michael is tired of the LEGO Network, he turns on his Xbox One and Xbox Live to connect to the rest of the world. Like most kids his age, Michael never plays video games by himself anymore. Instead, he signs on to the network and looks to see what games his neighborhood friends are already playing. He then responds to requests to join their games or invites them to join him. Many of the games that he plays require him to be part of a team and work toward defined goals with other people, mirroring the kinds of collaborative work done by his parents when they are at work.

If Michael had his choice, though, he would play *Rock Band* all day long. After he slips the game disc into his Xbox, he starts a band as the drummer—his favorite instrument—and waits for a guitar player, bassist, and singer. After a handful of digital friends join his band—sometimes people he knows from school and other times people he has just met online—they take turns picking songs and playing sets of music. While his parents have turned the game's chat feature off in order to keep Michael safe, he still enjoys jamming out with people all over the world. It didn't take long for Michael to become an expert at *Rock Band*—or for his developing love of music and performance to extend into the real world, where he now has his own drum kit sitting in the corner of his bedroom.

For the most part, Michael sees the Internet as a tool for staying connected and for finding information. He is still too young to join Facebook, but he does spend time messing around on kid-friendly social networks. While his interests are always changing—which explains the ten different social sites that he has explored—Webkinz (www.webkinz.com/us_en) and Club Penguin (www.clubpenguin.com) have kept his attention for a while now. Michael also likes to play learning games while he is online, but he doesn't think he is "learning" because he gets to pick the things he wants to study. His favorite has been DimensionM (www.dimensionm.com) created by Tabula Digita, which is teaching him algebra skills in an online video game environment. His parents are shocked because Michael refuses to give up when playing DimensionM. Instead, he turns to the help feature in the software to learn the math necessary to solve the problems that he can't figure out on his own and then goes back to mastering the level.

Michael does everything—from defining words and watching NFL highlights to designing virtual worlds and communicating with friends—online. His brain is wired to get information when he needs it and to use that information to solve problems or answer questions that are important to him. His network is vast, and he knows how to use it to direct his own learning.

Bridging the School and Home Gap

Without asking, Michael is also starting to bridge what he knows about technology with the work that he is doing at school. Recently, he was supposed to create a timeline detailing the lives of all of the presidents born in the Midwest. While this is a low-level thinking task, it could easily consume hours poking through stacks of encyclopedias in the public library. In fact, that's exactly what his teacher wanted: her stated goal for the project was to teach students to research.

What she didn't realize is that Michael wasn't about to give up an entire Saturday for schoolwork. He immediately turned to Google to assemble his data. After typing "U.S. Presidents" into the search box, Michael had an organized list of important information about every president. Then, he deleted all of the presidents that weren't born in the Midwest and sorted the eleven remaining presidents by birth date. He polished his writing—knowing that he had to put research facts into his own words—and emailed his final product to his teacher. The entire task took about ten minutes.

Michael's work was an "aha" moment for his teacher. She quickly realized that she was requiring students to master skills that were no longer needed. The kinds of information gathering and sorting that were once done by hand could easily be automated and customized by individual kids if they just knew which tools to use. At first, she was embarrassed to have fallen so far behind. She is beginning to understand that if digital tools could make students more efficient, there would be more free time in class to wrestle with the kinds of complex tasks—problem solving, communication, collaboration, persuasion—that she had pushed aside for so many years. *Twenty-first-century learning*, a buzzword that she had grown tired of, wasn't about replacing the work that she was already doing. Instead, it was about using digital tools to support and extend the kinds of cognitively challenging experiences that she cared about.

She knew, though, that making the most of digital tools was going to require structure and guidance on her part—she had seen too many examples of teachers who simply turned their students loose with blogs and wikis only to find that the quality of the work produced was appalling—and she was ready for the challenge. Immediately, she began experimenting with ways to expose her students to new experiences built around important concepts. She was determined to set high standards for her students and was convinced that she could find a way to pair what she knew about good teaching with what Michael and his peers knew about technology. Her efforts are a work in progress, but she has taken the all-important first step, and we are convinced that she will succeed!

Hearing From Michael

Knowing that we wanted to spotlight Michael's voice in the epilogue of *Teaching the iGeneration*, we asked him if he would be willing to write an essay describing an ideal vision of schooling that we could share with our readers. Jazzed by the thought of "being published," Michael worked for months, crafting his thinking in countless conversations and writing more drafts than he has ever written for a school project. He has become a polished little presenter who knows more than most about what schools could be—and his essay paints a pretty convincing vision that impressed us enough to include it in full:

> The first thing I would do is make sure that everyone had a laptop so that when they need information or to learn something they could go out to the Internet and get it. You wouldn't have to go to the school building every day, maybe two days a week you could work from home or a place where you could get on the Internet. On the days that you didn't go to school you would have to work for at least seven hours, but you could choose the hours that you wanted to work. For example, you could get up at six o'clock in the morning and work until noon, take a two hour break, and then work one more hour.
>
> We would learn by working on projects. Some of the projects I would complete by myself, but most of the time I would work on a team to complete the work. When I was at school the teacher would still organize our day and help choose the projects that we worked on. The teacher would also help us when we had difficulty learning something we need to know. When we completed the projects we have to present them to other students or teachers and that is how we get our grades.
>
> The Internet could be used for learning games and to communicate with people in my group. I could also work with kids that weren't on my grade level if I needed help or someone needed my help. School would be really cool, and I would just be learning all of the time. (M. Garry, personal communication, January 18, 2010)

Teaching the iGeneration was designed to present many examples of how Michael's idea of learning can become a reality. We hope that you find value in the projects, resources, and ideas that we have shared and work diligently to create the kinds of learning environments that meet the needs of digital learners.

Technology Permission Slip

Often, teachers and administrators feel uncomfortable about introducing digital tools to students because of Internet safety risks that are widely reported in the media. These fears are completely understandable! In fact, moving forward with digital projects before articulating specific actions that parents, teachers, and students should take to keep safe online would be nothing short of irresponsible. Teaching students strategies for self-protection is a basic requirement for any educator interested in using digital tools to facilitate instruction.

This document outlines both the reasons that digital tools should play a larger role in classroom instruction and the behaviors expected of parents, teachers, and students in 21st century classrooms. It can be used as a permission slip to generate commitment to Internet safety before digital projects are started.

Teaching the iGeneration

Dear Parents,

Perhaps the greatest challenge facing parents and teachers is preparing students for a future that is rapidly changing yet poorly defined. New content and information is constantly being created, new partnerships developed across global boundaries are becoming commonplace, and new tools are connecting workers who once would have remained isolated.

Put simply, the work world that your children will inherit will be dramatically different than the work world of today! To properly prepare our students for that reality, we are planning to incorporate new digital tools into learning experiences here at school this year. Specifically, your child may have opportunities to use the following.

- **Tools for content creation:** Today's students must recognize that in a world where new information is generated at a blinding pace, the ability to develop novel ideas after a careful process of synthesis and evaluation—and to edit and publish those ideas to wide audiences—is far more important than simply consuming knowledge generated by others.

- **Tools for communication:** Today's students must be able to engage in both collaborative and competitive dialogue. They must be able to understand different roles in complex networks of learners, respect multiple viewpoints, recognize how important listening is in productive conversations, and articulate a range of positions clearly. Today's students must learn to see communication as an opportunity to refine and revise their own thinking.

- **Tools for collaboration:** Because companies are becoming increasingly global, creating work teams of colleagues on different continents, it is imperative for students to begin collaborating with peers across classrooms, schools, communities, and oceans. They must be equal partners in the creation of documents and presentations and have ample opportunities to create shared final products. Ongoing experiences with collaborative exercises will help students learn the task management skills that are often prerequisites for successful participation in a world driven by joint endeavors.

- **Tools for information management:** Perhaps the greatest challenge facing today's students is sifting through the amazing amount of content being created and selecting what is truly useful. Where students of an earlier generation had access to a handful of sources while exploring new ideas, today's students have access to tens of thousands of sources. Students must learn to balance primary sources (interviews, blogs, surveys, personal data collection, and so on) with secondary sources (magazines, newspapers, websites, books, and so on) when collecting and organizing information.

Specifically, our students may be engaged in the following.

- **Reading and commenting on blogs being created by other students:** One of the best ways to motivate students to read is to provide them with opportunities to share their thinking with other students. Collections of classroom blogs make that possible. You can explore the blogs that your children will be exposed to by visiting this URL:

  _____

- **Creating a classroom wiki:** A wiki is an editable website that allows many writers to create content together. In education, wikis are generally used by students completing

page 1 of 4

classroom projects. At our school, wikis are only editable by students in our building or by students in sister schools that we work with closely. Generally, our wikis are closed to outsiders—however, there are times when wikis are opened to the world. Here is a sample of a public wiki created by middle school students: http://carbonfighters.pbworks.com.

- **Joining in digital conversations with other students:** Middle grade students are social by nature, completely driven by opportunities to interact in ongoing conversations with one another. At our school, we plan to tap into this motivation by creating digital conversations connected to classroom content.

  These conversations are always closely monitored by classroom teachers, and all comments are viewed by teachers before they can be seen by students. What's more, participation in our conversations is limited to students in our school or in sister schools that we partner with. Here is a sample conversation created by middle school students: http://ed.voicethread.com/share/62276.

- **Writing entries for our classroom blog:** Student writers are generally motivated by having an audience and receiving feedback from their peers. At our school, those goals are often accomplished by creating classroom blogs. Blogs are public websites on which students post content and readers from around the world leave comments.

  To ensure that inappropriate content is not added to classroom blogs, teachers review all new entries and comments before they are seen by students. What's more, students are taught to never reveal their full identity or their location. Here is a sample blog that has been maintained by middle school students: http://sugarkills.us.

Addressing Internet Safety

Students of the 21st century are exposed to different dangers than those faced by earlier generations. With nothing more than a few simple mouse clicks, children can stumble upon inappropriate content or participate in potentially unsafe interactions with other users.

Students must be skilled at self-advocacy and protection. They must learn to guard themselves and their identities while creating, communicating, and collaborating in virtual environments. They must recognize and have an action plan for removing themselves from dangerous situations. They must also understand and respect the line between one's public and private life.

Age-appropriate guidance, monitoring, and guidelines assist students as they learn to take responsibility for their own behavior when using online resources. Providing controlled educational environments focused on learning helps students utilize new tools responsibly while giving educators and parents the required safety and security.

To help prepare our students to be responsible digital citizens, we will consistently emphasize and enforce the following rules for Internet safety in our classrooms and community.

- **Students participating in any digital project are expected to act safely by keeping personal information private:** They are expected to never share their family names, passwords, usernames, email addresses, home addresses, school names, city names, or other information that could make identification possible.

- **Students participating in any digital project will let teachers or parents know when a digital interaction seems unsafe:** They are expected to help police their classroom projects by pointing out any inappropriate comments or interactions to parents or teachers.

- **Students participating in any digital project are expected to treat the project as a classroom space:** They understand that speech inappropriate for class is also inappropriate for our digital projects. If inappropriate language is posted in digital projects, students understand that they will be referred to the office for consequences. Students also understand that repeated instances of inappropriate language or content will result in the closing of all classroom projects.

- **Teachers understand that all content created by their students must be monitored and moderated:** A primary responsibility of all teachers interested in using digital tools in the classroom is ensuring student safety. The first step to making digital learning experiences safe is monitoring and moderating all content posted in digital projects. Teachers accept responsibility for reviewing and approving all comments added to blogs or digital conversations before they are made available to student readers. Teachers also accept responsibility for reviewing content created by students on an ongoing basis and closed projects that are no longer active.

- **Teachers take active steps to review Internet safety rules with students frequently throughout the course of the school year:** Teachers understand that students need consistent reminders and reinforcement about safe online behaviors. As a result, they regularly introduce short minilessons on digital safety in their classrooms. One website that is regularly used to develop minilessons is Common Sense Media: www.commonsensemedia.org/educators/curriculum.

- **Parents recognize that they have an obligation to monitor digital activities and behaviors beyond the school day:** The greatest risks to students engaged in digital projects come from unsupervised participation in online activities. While the faculty and staff will carefully monitor student involvement in classroom projects, parents understand that we cannot effectively monitor student activities beyond the school day or beyond the scope of school-sponsored activities.

  Therefore, parents accept responsibility for monitoring the online lives of their children away from our school. One of the first steps that proactive parents often take is ensuring that the family computer is in a public location, making monitoring easy!

- **Parents accept responsibility for learning more about Internet safety:** There are many resources available online that can be used by parents to learn more about keeping their children digitally safe. A growing collection of these resources can be explored by visiting the Family Toolbox created by Common Sense Media: www.commonsensemedia.org/educators/connecting-families/share.

Permission

Before your child may fully participate in our technology experiments, I am asking for you and your child to agree to the Internet safety rules and to acknowledge your consent by signing and returning the following form.

I have read and understood the rules for keeping students safe while working on digital projects. I agree to abide by each of the rules, doing my part to make digital learning experiences both fun *and* safe at our school.

Student Name (please print):

Student Signature: Date:

Parent's Signature: Date:

References and Resources

Ahuja, M. (2013, March 13). Teens are spending more time consuming media, on mobile devices. *Washington Post*. Accessed at www.washingtonpost.com/postlive/teens-are-spending-more-time-consuming-media-on -mobile-devices/2013/03/12/309bb242–8689–11e2–98a3-b3db6b9ac586_story.html on October 10, 2014.

Barseghian, T. (2012, August 31). What will you click on next? Focusing our attention online [Web log post]. Accessed at http://blogs.kqed.org/mindshift/2012/08/what-will-you-click-on-next-focusing-our-attention-online on October 21, 2014.

Bauerlein, M. (2008). *The dumbest generation: How the digital age stupefies young Americans and jeopardizes our future (or, don't trust anyone under 30)*. New York: Tarcher/Penguin.

Bettelheim, M. (2007, March 14). Tentacled tree hugger disarms seventh graders. *Inkling*. Accessed at www.inklingmagazine .com/articles/tentacled-tree-hugger-gets-legs-up-on-twelve-year-olds on January 21, 2010.

boyd, d. (2007). Why youth (heart) social network sites: The role of networked publics in teenage social life. In D. Buckingham (Ed.), *Youth, identity, and digital media* (pp. 119–142). Cambridge, MA: Massachusetts Institute of Technology Press.

boyd, d. (2008, January 15). The economist debate on social "networking" [Web log post]. Accessed at www.zephoria .org/thoughts/archives/2008/01/15/the_economist_d.html on August 20, 2009.

boyd, d. (2010). Friendship. In M. Ito, S. Baumer, M. Bittanti, d. boyd, R. Cody, et al., *Hanging out, messing around, and geeking out: Kids living and learning with new media* (pp. 79–115). Cambridge, MA: Massachusetts Institute of Technology Press.

Brown, D. (2005). The writing classroom as a laboratory for democracy: An interview with Don Rothman. *Higher Education Exchange*, 43–55.

Brown, G. (Speaker). (2009, July). *Wiring a web for global good* [Video file]. Accessed at www.ted.com/talks/gordon _brown.html on March 20, 2010.

Busteed, B. (2013, January 7). The school cliff: Student engagement drops with each school year [Web log post]. Accessed at http://thegallupblog.gallup.com/2013/01/the-school-cliff-student-engagement.html on October 10, 2014.

Cashmore, P. (2009, December 17). *YouTube: Why do we watch?* Accessed at www.cnn.com/2009/TECH/12/17/cashmore .youtube/index.html on January 21, 2010.

Common Sense Media. (2009). *Is social networking changing childhood? A national poll*. San Francisco: Author.

Cookson, P. W., Jr. (2009). What would Socrates say? *Educational Leadership, 67*(1), 8–14.

Copeland, M. (2005). *Socratic circles: Fostering critical and creative thinking in middle and high school*. Portland, ME: Stenhouse.

Creative Commons. (n.d.a). *About the licenses*. Accessed at http://creativecommons.org/about/licenses on January 21, 2010.

Creative Commons. (n.d.b). *History*. Accessed at http://creativecommons.org/about/history on January 21, 2010.

Cutler, D. (2013, August 23). *Changing the world with Challenge 20/20*. Accessed at www.spinedu.com/difference -challenge-2020/#.VFk142ctBHg on October 22, 2014.

Davidson, H. (2004, April 5). *Meaningful digital video for every classroom*. Accessed at www.techlearning.com /article/2166 on January 21, 2010.

Dewey, J. (1910). *How we think*. Boston: Heath.

Downey, M. (2014, August 6). *M-rated video games: M for mistake to let teens spend so much time playing them?* Accessed at www.ajc.com/weblogs/get-schooled/2014/aug/06/m-rated-video-games-m-mistake-let-teens-play-them on October 10, 2014.

Etherington, D. (2014, February 10). *Flickr at 10: 1M photos shared per day, 170% increase since making 1TB free*. Accessed at http://techcrunch.com/2014/02/10/flickr-at-10–1m-photos-shared-per-day-170-increase-since-making -1tb-free on October 27, 2014.

Ferriter, W. (2005, July 1). *Digital dialogue*. Accessed at www.techlearning.com/from-the-classroom/0015/digital -dialogue/42767 on January 21, 2010.

Ferriter, W. (2008, April 10). Statistically speaking . . . [Web log post]. Accessed at http://blog.williamferriter .com/2008/04/10/statistically-s on January 21, 2010.

Ferriter, W. (2009). Learning with blogs and wikis. *Educational Leadership, 66*(5), 34–38.

Foshay, R., & Kirkley, J. (2003). *Principles for teaching problem solving* (Technical Paper No. 4). Bloomington, MN: PLATO Learning.

Fox, S., & Rainie, L. (2014, February 27). *The web at 25 in the U.S.* Accessed at www.pewinternet.org/2014/02/27/the -web-at-25-in-the-u-s on October 11, 2014.

Fullan, M. (2013). *Stratosphere: Integrating technology, pedagogy, and change knowledge*. Dons Mills, Ontario, Canada: Pearson.

Getzels, J. W., & Csikszentmihalyi, M. (1967). Science creativity. *Science Journal, 3*(9), 80–84.

Getzels, J. W., & Csikszentmihalyi, M. (1976). *The creative vision: A longitudinal study of problem finding in art*. New York: Wiley.

Gillett, R. (2014, April 22). *How the most successful brands dominate Instagram, and you can too*. Accessed at www .fastcompany.com/3029395/bottom-line/how-the-most-successful-brands-dominate-instagram-and-you -can-too on October 27, 2014.

Gillies, J., & Cailliau, R. (2000). *How the web was born: The story of the World Wide Web*. New York: Oxford University Press.

Hampton, K. N., Sessions, L. F., Her, E. J., & Rainie, L. (2009). *Social isolation and new technology: How the Internet and mobile phones impact Americans' social networks*. Washington, DC: Pew Research Center.

Hargadon, S. (2009). *Educational networking: The important role Web 2.0 will play in education*. Pleasanton, CA: Elluminate.

Heath, C., & Heath, D. (2007). *Made to stick: Why some ideas survive and others die*. New York: Random House.

Helft, M. (2009, December 30). YouTube's quest to suggest more. *New York Times*. Accessed at www.nytimes .com/2009/12/31/technology/internet/31tube.html?_r=1&ref=media on January 21, 2010.

Hess, F. M. (2008). *Still at risk: What students don't know, even now.* Washington, DC: Common Core.

Horst, H. A., Herr-Stephenson, B., & Robinson, L. (2010). Media ecologies. In M. Ito, S. Baumer, M. Bittanti, d. boyd, R. Cody, et al., *Hanging out, messing around, and geeking out: Kids living and learning with new media* (pp. 29–78). Cambridge, MA: Massachusetts Institute of Technology Press.

Huston, T. (2009, May 31). Making sense of the dumbest generation. *Huffington Post.* Accessed at www.huffingtonpost .com/tom-huston/making-sense-of-the-dumbe_b_192948.html on August 31, 2009.

Instagram. (n.d.). *Press page.* Accessed at http://instagram.com/press on October 27, 2014.

International Society for Technology in Education. (n.d.). *ISTE Standards: Students.* Accessed at www.iste.org/docs /pdfs/20-14_ISTE_Standards-S_PDF.pdf on October 27, 2014.

Ito, M., Horst, H., Bittanti, M., boyd, d., Herr-Stephenson, B., Lange, P. G., et al. (2009). *Living and learning with new media: Summary of findings from the Digital Youth Project.* Cambridge, MA: Massachusetts Institute of Technology Press.

Koetsier, J. (2013, March 1). *How Google searches 30 trillion web pages, 100 billion times a month.* Accessed at http:// venturebeat.com/2013/03/01/how-google-searches-30-trillion-web-pages-100-billion-times-a-month on October 10, 2014.

Krane, B. (2006, November 13). Researchers find kids need better online academic skills. *UConn Advance, 25*(12). Accessed at http://advance.uconn.edu/2006/061113/06111308.htm on January 21, 2010.

Kubicek, J. (2014, June 17). *2014 Teen Choice Award nominations: "TVD" and "PLL" top all shows.* Accessed at www .buddytv.com/articles/pretty-little-liars/2014-teen-choice-award-nominat-53843.aspx on October 10, 2014.

Lenhart, A., & Madden, M. (2007). *Social networking websites and teens: An overview.* Washington, DC: Pew Research Center.

Lerner, G. (2012, September 14). *New York health board approves ban on large sodas.* Accessed at www.cnn.com/2012/09/13 /health/new-york-soda-ban on October 12, 2014.

Li, C., & Bernoff, J. (2008). *Groundswell: Winning in a world transformed by social technologies.* Boston: Harvard Business Press.

Lipsman, A. (2009, March 4). *YouTube surpasses 100 million U.S. viewers for the first time* [Press release]. Accessed at www.comscore.com/Press_Events/Press_Releases/2009/3/YouTube_Surpasses_100_Million_US_Viewers on January 21, 2010.

Lipsman, A. (2010, January 5). *November sees number of U.S. videos viewed online surpass 30 billion for first time on record* [Press release]. Accessed at www.comscore.com/Press_Events/Press_Releases/2010/1/November_Sees _Number_of_U.S._Videos_Viewed_Online_Surpass_30_Billion_for_First_Time_on_Record on January 21, 2010.

Madden, M. (2007). *Online videos go mainstream: Most Internet users—and three-in four-young adults—now watch them.* Washington, DC: Pew Research Center.

Madden, M. (2013, August 15). *Teens haven't abandoned Facebook (yet).* Accessed at www.pewinternet.org/2013/08/15 /teens-havent-abandoned-facebook-yet on October 10, 2014.

Madden, M., Lenhart, A., Cortesi, S., Gasser, U., Duggan, M., Smith, A., et al. (2013). *Teens, social media, and privacy.* Washington, DC: Pew Research Center.

McKinsey & Company. (2009). *The economic impact of the achievement gap in America's schools.* New York: Author.

Meeker, M. (2013, May 29). *2013 Internet trends.* Accessed at www.kpcb.com/insights/2013-internet-trends on October 27, 2014.

MiddleWeb. (2013, March 17). *Interview: The #SUGARKILLS gang*. Accessed at www.middleweb.com/6563/interview-the-sugarkills-gang on October 12, 2014.

Mike. (2007, April 7). Re: Another failed "shock and awe" campaign [Web log comment]. Accessed at http://blog.williamferriter.com/2007/04/06/a_report_releas on January 21, 2010.

National Association for Sport and Physical Education. (2004). *Moving into the future: National standards for physical education* (2nd ed.). Reston, VA: Author.

National Association of Independent Schools. (2014, March 4). *Challenge 20/20*. Accessed at www.nais.org/Articles/Pages/Challenge-20–20.aspx on November 5, 2014.

National Center for Education Statistics. (2013). *Are the nation's 12th-graders making progress in mathematics and reading?* Accessed at http://nces.ed.gov/nationsreportcard/subject/publications/main2013/pdf/2014087.pdf on October 10, 2014.

National Council for the Social Studies. (2010). *National curriculum standards for social studies*. Silver Spring, MD: Author.

National Council of Teachers of English. (2013). *NCTE framework for 21st century curriculum and assessment*. Accessed at www.ncte.org/positions/statements/21stcentframework on October 10, 2014.

National Council of Teachers of Mathematics. (2004). *Principles and standards for school mathematics*. Reston, VA: Author.

National Education Association. (2008). *Access, adequacy, and equity in education technology: Results of a survey of America's teachers and support professionals on technology in public schools and classrooms*. Washington, DC: Author.

National Governors Association Center for Best Practices & Council of Chief State School Officers. (2010). *Common Core State Standards for English language arts and literacy in History/Social Studies, Science, and Technical Subjects*. Washington, DC: Authors. Accessed at www.corestandards.org/wp-content/uploads/ELA_Standards.pdf on December 16, 2014.

Newman, A. A. (2009, October 28). A campaign for clothes by a guy not wearing any. *New York Times*. Accessed at www.nytimes.com/2009/10/29/business/media/29zappos.html on January 21, 2010.

NGSS Lead States. (2013). *Next Generation Science Standards: For states, by states*. Washington, DC: National Academies Press.

Norris, P. (2001). *Digital divide: Civic engagement, information poverty, and the Internet worldwide*. New York: Cambridge University Press.

Oblinger, D. G., & Oblinger, J. L. (Eds.). (2005). *Educating the net generation*. Boulder, CO: EDUCAUSE.

Partnership for 21st Century Skills. (2009). *Framework for 21st century learning*. Accessed at www.p21.org/about-us/p21-framework on January 13, 2015.

Partnership for 21st Century Skills. (2012). *High schools must integrate framework for 21st century learning to produce effective citizens in a global economy*. Accessed at www.p21.org/news-events/press-releases/202-high-schools-must-integrate-framework-for-21st-century-learning-to-produce-effective-citizens-in-a-global-economy on January 13, 2015.

Patterson, K., Grenny, J., Maxfield, D., McMillan, R., & Switzler, A. (2008). *Influencer: The power to change anything*. New York: McGraw-Hill.

Pew Research Center. (2012). *Teens fact sheet*. Accessed at www.pewinternet.org/fact-sheets/teens-fact-sheet on October 10, 2014.

Prensky, M. (2009, July 12). Re: The larger lessons [Web log comment]. Accessed at http://weblogg-ed.com/2009 /the-larger-lessons/#comment-70619 on July 19, 2009.

Rapaport, R. (2009, October 27). *The new literacy: Scenes from the digital divide 2.0.* Accessed at www.edutopia.org /digital-generation-divide-literacy on January 21, 2010.

Rheingold, H. (2012). *Net smart: How to thrive online.* Cambridge, MA: Massachusetts Institute of Technology.

Richardson, W. (2008, February 14). What do we know about our kids' futures? Really [Web log post]. Accessed at http://weblogg-ed.com/2008/what-do-we-know-about-our-kids-futures-really on July 19, 2009.

Richardson, W. (2009, April 22). New reading, new writing [Web log post]. Accessed at http://weblogg-ed.com/2009 /new-reading-new-writing on January 21, 2010.

Richardson, W. (2012). *Why school?: How education must change when learning and information are everywhere.* New York: TED Conferences.

Rideout, V. J., Foehr, U. G., & Roberts, D. F. (2010). *Generation M²: Media in the lives of 8- to 18-year-olds.* Menlo Park, CA: Kaiser Family Foundation.

Sage, A. (2009, November 16). Evian roller babies attract record 45m hits. *The Times.* Accessed at www.thetimes.co.uk /tto/technology/article1859792.ece on January 21, 2010.

Samuels, H. (2009). *Focusing a research topic.* Accessed at www.crlsresearchguide.org/08_focusing_a_topic.asp on January 21, 2010.

Santa, C. M., Havens, L. T., & Valdes, B. J. (2004). *Project CRISS: Creating independence through student-owned strategies* (3rd ed.). Dubuque, IA: Kendall/Hunt.

Shirky, C. (2002, October 3). *Weblogs and the mass amateurization of publishing* [Electronic mailing list message]. Accessed at www.shirky.com/writings/weblogs_publishing.html on January 21, 2010.

Smith, C. (2013, September 18). Facebook users are uploading 350 million new photos each day. *Business Insider.* Accessed at www.businessinsider.com/facebook-350-million-photos-each-day-2013–9 on October 29, 2014.

Smith, R. A. (2009, December 31).Two dowdy clothing brands go for vogue. *Wall Street Journal.* Accessed at http://online .wsj.com/article/SB10001424052748703510304574626740978607998.html?mod=djemPJ on January 21, 2010.

Surowiecki, J. (2004). *The wisdom of crowds: Why the many are smarter than the few and how collective wisdom shapes business, economies, societies, and nations.* New York: Doubleday.

Tapscott, D. (1998). *Growing up digital: The rise of the net generation.* New York: McGraw-Hill.

Tapscott, D. (2009). *Grown up digital: How the net generation is changing your world.* New York: McGraw-Hill.

Tapscott, D., & Williams, A. D. (2006). *Wikinomics: How mass collaboration changes everything.* New York: Portfolio.

Thompson, D. (2014, June 19). The most popular social network for young people? Texting. *The Atlantic.* Accessed at www.theatlantic.com/technology/archive/2014/06/facebook-texting-teens-instagram-snapchat-most -popular-social-network/373043 on October 10, 2014.

Three loud cheers for the father of the web. (2005, January 28). *The Telegraph.* Accessed at www.telegraph.co.uk/news /uknews/1482211/Three-loud-cheers-for-the-father-of-the-web.html on January 21, 2010.

TOTEMS. (n.d.). *Instagram statistics.* Accessed at http://totems.co/instagram-statistics on October 27, 2014.

YouTube. (n.d.). *Statistics.* Accessed at www.youtube.com/yt/press/statistics.html on October 16, 2014.

Index

Building a Professional Learning Community at Work™ : A Guide to the First Year
Parry Graham and William M. Ferriter
Foreword by Richard DuFour and Rebecca DuFour
This play-by-play guide to implementing PLC concepts uses a story to focus each chapter. The authors analyze the story, highlighting good decisions and mistakes. They offer research behind best practice and wrap up each chapter with practical recommendations and tools. **BKF273**

21st Century Skills: Rethinking How Students Learn
Edited by James Bellanca and Ron Brandt
This book introduces the 21st century skills movement, the Partnership for 21st Century Skills, and the Framework for 21st Century Learning. Chapters focus on why these skills are necessary, which are most important, and how to best help schools include them in their repertoire. **BKF389**

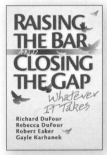

Raising the Bar and Closing the Gap: Whatever It Takes
Richard DuFour, Rebecca DuFour, Robert Eaker, and Gayle Karhanek
This sequel to the best-selling *Whatever It Takes: How Professional Learning Communities Respond When Kids Don't Learn* expands on original ideas and presses further with new insights. Foundational concepts combine with real-life examples of schools throughout North America that have gone from traditional cultures to PLCs. **BKF378**

On Excellence in Teaching
Edited by Robert Marzano
Learn from the world's best education researchers, theorists, and staff developers. The authors' diverse expertise delivers a wide range of theories and strategies and provides a comprehensive view of effective instruction from a theoretical, systemic, and classroom perspective. **BKF278**

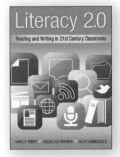

Literacy 2.0: Reading and Writing in 21st Century Classrooms
Nancy Frey, Douglas Fisher, and Alex Gonzalez
Literacy 2.0 is where traditional literacy and technological literacy meet. Benefit from the authors' extensive experience in secondary literacy 2.0 classrooms. Discover precisely what students need to be taught to become proficient in the literacies associated with information and communication technologies. **BKF373**

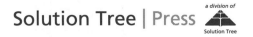

Visit solution-tree.com or call 800.733.6786 to order.